WisingUp is ([...] t it's
an easy read.... [...] tify
role models... to be[come] the best that he [or she] can be.

> Hanna Fernando, 21, Youth Leader, the Philippines

A collection of sayings from many cultures, *WisingUp* juxtaposes
such suggestions as "Go for It!" with "Wait a Minute!" As a result,
the reader finds support in the internal search for wisdom.

> Emilyn Inglis, 24, Oberlin College Graduate, USA

This book is amazing! I like how it's a little guide for young people,
something that was made especially for us. I would recommend this
book for all youth. Not only that, but it can also provide helpful
reminders for adults.

> Hapistinna Grace Horne, 19, Enrolled Member of
> the Sisseton-Wahpeton Oyate; Founder, Wolakota
> Youth Council, USA

This book is an extremely refreshing read, something every young
person (and young at heart) should have the opportunity to go through,
especially in this day and age. One realizes that what they read they
already know, but with the world moving and changing so fast around
us, sometimes it needs to be brought to the fore for us to remember.

> Vera Akatsa-Bukachi, 21, Kenya, National
> Representative to the World Congress of Youth,
> 2003, Morocco

An eye-opening, carefully selected list of 80 principles for good living.
This very special book is surely an investment worth making. A must for
every young person to read.

> Piotr Umha, 24, Secretary General,
> Polish Youth Council

This book stimulates reflection, as wrapped in its pages are the treasures and hopes of a soon-to-come change. A wise man once told me, "Change is in our youth. Old habits never die, so fix the new ones...." In my opinion, *WisingUp* can represent a step forward in this direction for humanity.

Rada Halaseh, 19, Youth Representative of the Women's Organization to Combat Illiteracy, Jordan

This book presents a wonderful constellation of wisdom and acts as an insightful guide for youth in the world today to navigate the difficult choices facing them with energy, compassion, and confidence.

Jonathan Kent Mitchell, 21, Youth Activist with WorldVoices, England, and Undergraduate, Cornell University, USA

WisingUp is an intoxicating read—fast paced, humorous, and most importantly, a call to common humanity. Anybody, regardless of background, experience and age, can use these short, eloquent chapters to guide thoughts and actions. I will certainly use them myself and with the young people I work with.

Nina O'Farrell, 23, Youth Officer, United Kingdom

WisingUp: A Youth Guide to Good Living provides a roadmap to higher awareness and consciousness, conveyed in an eloquent and profoundly written style. The book inspires and activates the human spirit. A must read for young and old alike.

Daniel Dubie, Producer-Director of the award-winning film "Souls at Bay," Thailand

Most of us take a lifetime to develop wisdom, but this book provides young people with a rich resource of the world's wisdom to tap into when needed. A great gift for a graduate or someone setting off on a journey.

Solihin and Alicia Thom, Co-authors of *Being Human: Exploring the Forces That Shape Us and Awaken an Inner Life*, Portland, Oregon, USA, 2003

Wising UP

A Youth Guide
to Good Living

Reynold Feldman & M. Jan Rumi

*For
Olivia,
Tanto gusto en
conocerti,
Reynold Ruslan
Freiburg, 28.7.2018*

WISDOM FOUNDATION PUBLISHING

WisingUp: A Youth Guide to Good Living

ISBN 1-932590-02-1

Published by
Wisdom Foundation Publishing
PO Box 61599
Honolulu, Hawaii 96839
USA

Phone: 808-988-4191
Fax: 808-988-4212

www.WisingUp.com
info@WisingUp.com

Please contact the publisher for organization bulk
orders of WisingUp.

1   2   3   4   5   6   7   8   9   10

Wising UP
A Youth Guide to Good Living

This book is dedicated to the youth of the world.

May it help them

have the wisdom they'll need

to live happy, meaningful lives

in solidarity

with others,

the Planet, and

the Great Spirit of the Universe.

Foreword

If school and university sports clubs are the lifeline for professional sports teams, then surely our Youth are the lifeline for society. As important to our survival as they are, however, they are the most under-served and under-represented segment of our society. The only time we show genuine interest in them, it seems, is when we want to sell them products that will not add value to their lives but line the pockets of those who sell them. Well, I believe this book, *WisingUp: A Youth Guide To Good Living*, has the potential to change that.

WisingUp deals with everyday issues in a crisp, easy-to-read, common-sense manner. It speaks to our young people in a respectful manner. It does not give sermons. It incorporates the wisdom of the sages and the ages. As I read it, I got the feeling that the authors, Reynold Feldman and Jan Rumi, wrote it with compassion and a deep sense of love for our young citizens. I truly believe that *WisingUp* is an antidote to the streams of negative images young people receive every day. In a world where so many adults are looking to use young people, *WisingUp* is a guide to help them create better lives for themselves.

We all know it's not possible to force anyone, especially youth, to do something, regardless how beneficial it may be. However, I do feel it is the responsibility of all adults to find ways to encourage every young person they know to read this book. There are many stories of youth who have reversed their attitudes from negative to positive. Frequently these stories have to do with concerned adults who demonstrated in a meaningful way that they really

cared. Sharing this book could be your way to demonstrate that you care. By doing so, you have the potential to nourish our school teams for life and thereby save the world.

Thank you and aloha,

Wally Amos
Honolulu, Hawai'i • February, 2004

Preface

Why this book now?

The world is in a crisis of rebirth. Either the human family learns how to live and work together in peace and harmony, or we might not reach the 22nd Century. Mother and child may die.

The good news is, there are organizations and individuals emerging on the Planet each day with an unstoppable desire to end all the isms, stop the violence, respect natural systems, and focus on our true work of eradicating hunger, poverty, disease, and ignorance. In other words, the child to be born shows great promise. Our job as godparents is to make sure that it grows to adulthood.

We write these words after returning from participating in an event of great importance: The World Congress of Youth in Morocco. There some 1,000 young people, 15 to 25 years old, from 144 countries spent two weeks together in the cause of Solidarity, Tolerance, and Sustainable Development. Two hundred of us adult observers attended as well. The big lesson of the Congress was that a new generation of leaders is poised to play their role in the world. Now it is up to us, their seniors, to share what wisdom we have as they prepare for their all-important responsibility.

This little book is our attempt to do just that. Coming from a Jewish-Christian and a Muslim background, one from the United States, the other from Bangladesh, we hope we can model the kind of unlikely collaboration the world now requires in growing numbers to survive and

thrive. At the same time, we intend that the 80 often-paradoxical principles we put forward will both give our new leaders the skills, attitudes, and behaviors needed to pilot Spaceship Earth safely to the next century and help them lead what has often been termed "the good life." We don't see these goals as mutually exclusive. Instead, as we assert in the Conclusion, it's all a matter of balance.

Finally, we hope this book will eventually get into the hands of youth around the world. First, because it will take a critical mass of the world's emerging leaders to pull off the sort of personal and societal transformation we have in mind. But as importantly, we intend to use the proceeds from *WisingUp* to fund youth-based and youth-oriented initiatives globally.

As we view the world situation today from a combined age of 111 years, there is only one race we hope will be won: the human race. If this thin volume does anything toward that end, we will have satisfied our mission.

Reynold Feldman and M. Jan Rumi
Honolulu, Hawai'i • March 2004

Introduction

Living well is the best revenge.
Hillel, d. 10 C.E.

Dear Youth of the World,

What is the good life, and how do you live it? This question has challenged humankind from the dawn of civilization.

Fortunately, the great sages, scholars, and poets of the world have offered answers, which, thanks to literacy, the invention of public libraries, and the patient labor of translators are now available to the great bulk of the human race, if they care to look. Collectively, these answers are known as wisdom. Yet few people nowadays have the time or discipline to read through the great works of ancient and modern philosophy and religion. Therefore, in this book we hope to supply that wisdom in 80 principles for good living that you can apply every day.

Be advised. There is nothing new here. Wisdom is as old as the hills. Every tradition has it. Every human being can prosper by it. In this book we have attempted to make the world's wisdom available to you in words you can understand and ways you can use. This advice is as valid now as ever. The only difference is, today we have access to everyone's wisdom, not just that of our group.

Of course, even the best advice is useless unless taken. So, read these pages, try what appeals to you, and leave the rest. Also, let us know what has worked for you and what hasn't. Your wisdom may help us produce a better edition of this book later.

We live in times of rapid, even cataclysmic change. May this little book help you steady your boat in even the roughest seas. Bon voyage!

User's Guide
Suggestions for Getting the
Most from This Book

You get out of something what you put into it.
Anglo-American Saying

Most of us read books casually. What benefits we derive—
of pleasure or instruction—come pretty much by themselves
and without fanfare. At the end we may say to ourselves,
"That was a good read." Or, "That was a waste of time."
Or maybe, "That book was pretty good—I think I got
something out of it." Many of you may read *WisingUp* in
this way. We hope you will find it rewarding.

Still, there are other ways of using this book, and since it
is a self-improvement manual, we would like to describe
them briefly. Also, *WisingUp* has been designed with
small-group and classroom instruction in mind, so, we will
include some suggestions below for peer leaders, teachers,
and youth workers as well.

WisingUp **as a Self-Help Manual.** Each of the eighty mini-
chapters contains "Optional Exercises," typically three. For
one thing, you could do the exercises, at least for those topics
where you feel the need to improve. Of course, if you believe
each of us could stand some improvement across the board,
you could go through the whole book and do some or all of
the exercises: perhaps only one or two in areas of strength and
all three where you feel you are weaker. Before beginning this
undertaking, you might write yourself a letter in which you
assess your personal strengths and weaknesses. Then after
completing the book and the exercises, you would review that

letter and write a new one commenting on what improvements you have made as well as areas that still need work.

While these letters and the written exercises can be filed in a simple manila folder, some of you might prefer to create a special journal where both letters and all the exercises could be kept together in chronological order. You might want to entitle the journal something like "My Self-Improvement Journal – 2005." Make sure to have a plan for keeping your journal safe and private. For if it is readily available for all to look through, you may be less willing to be honest with yourself—an important pre-condition for self-improvement.

WisingUp **and Tea for Two.** The title of a famous American popular song suggests another important way you can use this book: mutual self-help. You can work with a close friend or life partner. The term mutual is important here. Each of you should agree to work on him- or herself, then to meet periodically to share, over tea or coffee, what you have written and discuss how your "programs" are coming. To be sure, some of the exercises already ask you to interview a friend on a particular topic. What is suggested here is to share all (or at least most) of your work with someone else and to have that person share all her or his work with you.

Working with a Wisdom Coach. In this scenario we propose that you find an individual whom you respect to meet with you periodically to review your writings, do the oral exercises when called for, and basically to coach or mentor you through the book. This option is like the last one except that only you will be doing the exercises. The other person, the wisdom coach, will review them, provide a listening ear, and offer his or her comments in a careful, clear, yet diplomatic manner. The trick is to choose your wisdom coach wisely. It can be a favorite

uncle or aunt, a grandparent, teacher, sibling, or friend. Whether or not any payment for service takes place is up to the two of you. It is not recommended to pay friends or relatives; however, you might agree to take them out for coffee, tea, or a meal every once in a while in exchange for the time and effort they are expending. The situation with professionals—teachers, counselors, members of the clergy, etc.—is different. Do what is acceptable in your society in such cases, including monetary payment if that is appropriate.

WisingUp as a Peer-Group Activity. Some of you will belong to community, school, or religiously affiliated clubs or youth groups. You may want to consider working through *WisingUp* with three, four, or more people from one of those groups. If the study group gets larger—up to ten or twelve, say—you can always break up into smaller groups for sharing your work. It may take too much time and effort to share everything with everybody. If you vary the small-group membership from time to time, you will eventually get to know everyone better. Also, there is no requirement to do all the exercises for all the principles. The group could decide on spending a few weeks going through each person's favorite mini-chapter and doing only its exercises. Regardless of how long your group spends working through *WisingUp*, you'll notice how doing these exercises together will forge deeper bonds of friendship and community.

WisingUp as a Classroom Activity. One of us spent years teaching first-year (freshman) composition courses at universities. He also experimented with combining this introductory writing course with an orientation-to-college program. The results were sufficiently successful that other instructors began to copy his example. *WisingUp* was actually written as a possible text for use in high-school

English and college composition courses. Students improve their writing by writing, just as musicians improve their playing by practicing. What one writes about is less important. In this case, though, the writing (and discussion) would be on a topic near and dear to the hearts of all students—figuring out who they are and how they would like to live their lives. So, to high-school and university teachers reviewing this book, please consider how you might use it in composition and/or introduction-to-university courses. Again, not every chapter and exercise would need to be used. Pick and choose as you deem appropriate.

In fact, deciding on what should be used might be an excellent way to begin your course. As an initial assignment, ask the students to spend an hour skimming through the entire book. They should then pick out chapters and exercises they would most like to work through. Their reflection would be the basis for classroom discussion and decision-making. Of course, you as teachers may want to argue for inclusion or exclusion of certain materials for reasons of your own. The opportunity for practicing democracy—open covenants openly arrived at—is fairly obvious.

In one sense, our chapters and exercises are like pieces in a Lego set. How you determine to use them will reflect your creativity as a classroom instructor or as a class. There are also plenty of opportunities for small group or one-on-one work and for posting student papers around the room from time to time—so long as everyone is comfortable with this sort of "publication"—and giving all participants the opportunity to read what their classmates have written on a particular exercise. Some powerful peer learning can result from this activity. In addition, the book may lend itself to lively discussions

on the various topics—friendship, listening, laughing, moderation, etc.

One exercise not in the book which you may like to try is implied in the subtitle: *A Youth Guide to Good Living*. What is the good life? What does it entail, and how does one live it? As an assignment, ask the students in your class to write a letter to someone else. The person can be real or imaginary (such as a future grandchild). The students would advise the intended recipient on how to live "the good life." In class, small groups of four, say, would read their papers out loud to each other, then decide on having one paper from their group read to the whole class. After these readings—time permitting—students would be encouraged to brainstorm (shout out) the main characteristics of the good life, which you as teacher would number and list on the board. The challenge for you would be to combine closely related terms to avoid duplication. Next, ask students to vote on what they consider the five most important items. After tabulating the results, if there is any time left (or perhaps at the beginning of the next class), lead a mini-class discussion where students can comment on the highest-priority characteristics selected by class vote. You might do this exercise twice—once at the beginning and again at the end of the term or that portion of the term allotted to *WisingUp*.

The above are just some of the more intentional ways *WisingUp: A Youth Guide to Good Living* can be used for personal improvement and for creating a personally satisfying and meaningful life. Youth reading this book, teachers, youth workers, and others will doubtless come up with other ways. Our purpose is to be suggestive, not exhaustive.

We hope *WisingUp* serves you well. Please contact us through our website (www.WisingUp.com) with any suggestions or comments you may have. In the end, this book is like powdered milk, usable only if you add water and stir. Good luck.

Good-Living
Principles

1 Go for It!

The Hebrew Scriptures begin with an act of God. Not the kind insurance companies refer to. (Why don't they say "acts of Satan"?) The first thing the Bible reports is an action. God began everything by doing something. So can you.

Don't just stand there. Do something. Anything. Get on with it. Hamlet was a tragedy because the hero waited too long to take action. Do it now! Go for it!

What if you do the wrong thing? Make a mistake? Learn from it. Progress is a series of mistakes humanity has learned from. How can you get it right if you never get it wrong?

Even God seems to make mistakes the first time round. Think of the Garden of Eden and the Snake. Why in Christian tradition was Jesus' birth and death necessary, not to men-tion the Second Coming? God does things, reacts to changes, then does something new in response. So can you.

"Grow old along with me. / The best is yet to be," says Robert Browning's Rabbi Ben Ezra.

Take action. The life of wisdom is a life of deeds. It's up to you. Just do it.

> **Good-Living Principle 1:**
> **WISE UP by doing something**

Optional Exercises

1. Write about the dumbest thing you ever did and what you learned from it.

2. What action should you be taking in your life right now? Why aren't you? What do you need to do to get on with it?

3. What was the best thing you ever did? Why? How did the idea come to you, and where did you get the courage to carry it out? What were the benefits for yourself and others of doing this thing?

2 Wait a Minute!

> Don't just
> do something.
> Stand there.
>
> *American saying*

"Look before you leap" is one of the best-known proverbs in English. Why? Because people do lots of dumb things. They jump in without thinking about the consequences. They buy houses in flood plains, have unsafe sex, acquire a business without due diligence. Then they suffer as a result.

We know, we know. He who hesitates is lost. But a minute is not a year or a century. Take that breath. Think things over. Sleep on it. If it was good yesterday, it should be just as good tomorrow. If not, you'll be happy you waited. A stitch in time saves nine.

Remember to doubt. Girls who believe everything people tell them get pregnant when they thought they wouldn't. A little caution is a good thing, although a lot may keep you grounded forever.

Learn first, then fly with your

instructor, then work the simulator, then solo. Everything in due course. Step by step. One step at a time. One day at a time.

Eat the jello when it's jelled. Timing is everything. So remember to stop, look, and listen. Check first. Haste makes waste. Walking will often get you there faster than running. In short, don't just do something. Stand there.

> **Good-Living Principle 2:**
> **WISE UP by waiting a minute.**

Optional Exercises

1. Write three suggestions in your journal to keep yourself from making overly hasty decisions.

2. What difficult decision or action are you facing now? What sorts of things do you need to consider or do before you take that final step? Why?

3. Talk with the most successful person you know. Ask her or him what they do to assure that their initiatives come out well.

3 Take the Middle Way

> Avoid the extremes, O monks. Take the middle way.
>
> *A saying of the Buddha*

Nothing too much. Everything in moderation. Take moderation in moderation too. Sometimes you have to let your hair down. Sometimes you have to be as passive as a monk in a cell. Mostly, though, you have to follow the middle way. Eat your steaks medium. Be a vegetarian, but remember to include enough protein. Eat your fill but don't pig out.

Life is a balancing act. Work and pleasure. Being serious and being silly. Remembering others but not forgetting yourself. Handling the outer life but not forgetting the inner one.

The Buddha urged his monks and nuns to follow the Middle Way between self-denial and hedonism. The extremes were to be avoided. Aristotle, the Greek philosopher, said that virtues are always the middle option between too much and too little. Too much courage is foolhardiness. Too little is cowardice.

Once upon a time there was a king named Midas. He loved gold above all else and wished that everything he touched would turn to gold. Unfortunately, his dream came true. Consequently, he could no longer eat fruit or kiss his wife, for they would immediately be transformed. This was the result of his obsession.

Follow the way of the sages. Be moderate in everything, even your moderation.

Good-Living Principle 3:
WISE UP by taking the middle way.

Optional Exercise

1. Write about something extreme you once did. Would you do it again? Why? Why not?

2. Think about all the people you know fairly well. Who would be a role model for moderation? Write briefly about her or him.

3. Write a set of "Ten Commandments" for yourself to help you live a balanced, moderate life.

4 Keep It Simple

The hardest thing is to keep things simple. Simplicity of line, basic black, elegance. Yet we like to make things complicated, dress them up, go for the nuance Why? Who knows? Something about the temptation of Eden, maybe.

"Hear, O Israel, the Lord thy God, the Lord is one." That's the basic prayer of the Jewish people. Muslims say something similar. "There is no God but God." By contrast in the Christian Testament it is implied that Satan is legion—many.

When we are forced out of the womb—our personal Eden—we arrive in a world of complexity. In the beginning everything is done for us. Before long, though, we have to start doing things for ourselves. Eating food, putting on shoes, getting dressed, learning a profession, supporting ourselves. Womb service becomes for many of us a memory of paradise lost.

Others around us have needs too.
Sometimes theirs conflict with ours.
They want the toy we are playing
with, and they want it now. Help!

From simplicity to complexity to a
higher simplicity. Simplicity is no longer a given. Now we have to keep
things simple. Not simple-minded. Not
simplistic. Simple.

Simplify, simplify. Voluntary simplicity. Scale down. Scale back. Decrease
wants. Fulfill needs.

We live now. But we will die. Happy
Birthday! Happy New Year! Life is
short. So, what's important?

Think about it now. Feel about it now.
But don't get stressed. Keep it simple!

Good-Living Principle 4:
WISE UP by keeping it simple.

Optional Exercises

1. Where is my life most cluttered with
   complexity?

2. What three things could I do to simplify my life right now?

3. Journal about the best strategy to
   keep it simple.

5 Stay the Course

A little ax can cut down a big tree.
Jamaican Proverb

Perseverance may be the most under-rated virtue. It doesn't have the flash of heroism or the religious overtones of self-denial. But most of the world's work gets done through dogged persistence—by hanging in there until the job gets done.

The ancient Greeks had a saying: The gods sell all things to hard labor. Taoist philosophy points out how water, the most yielding of elements, can eventually wear away a rock. It's a matter of time and repetition.

A work begun may be half done. But persevering is all about the second half. Marathoners talk about hitting the wall. That's when the legs just don't want to keep working. Yet finishing is about staying the course to the end no matter what.

The smallest axes can cut down the largest trees, eventually. Skill plays a role. But it's perseverance that gets the job done.

Muslims are required to fast once a year for a month. Of course, they go without food and drink during only the daylight hours of each day. Still, the Ramadan fast can be a challenge. Again, it's a matter of staying the course and reaping the many benefits.

Awaiting the long-term results of hard work may not be the first choice in our age of instant gratification. Yet this ancient formula remains crucial for thriving in the 21st Century.

> **Good-Living Principle 5:**
> **WISE UP by staying the course.**

Optional Exercises

1. Write about an instance where you completed something difficult by persevering.

2. What are your biggest obstacles to completing major projects?

3. Pretend you'll be doing a marathon. Discuss your likely training program with a friend or colleague, or else draft a plan in your journal.

6 Take It Easy

The Twelve Step Program is full of wisdom. Much is encapsulated in the slogans. "One day at a time," "first things first," and "let go and let God" are three examples. As it happens, there are twelve.

"Take it easy" probably tops the bumper-sticker hit parade. The road, especially during rush hour, is a good place for this reminder. Life is short but the ride home frequently isn't. Road rage lurks around the corner— if you can ever get there. Don't stress. Don't explode. Take it easy.

You've got three things to do and time for only one. Your best friend calls. She's missed the bus. She's crying. "Jane, can you pick me up? Right now? Please!" Get your keys. Start the car. Cool your jets. Take it easy.

You're a working student. Your employer is having financial difficulties. They have to lay you off. Jobs are tight, and you have regular bills to pay. Don't worry. Don't go crazy. Take it easy.

Life is full of ups and downs. Learn to take things as they come. Give everything your best shot. But if all else fails, don't fret. Don't sweat. Remember to apply these magic words: Take it easy.

> **Good-Living Principle 6:**
> **WISE UP by taking it easy.**

Optional Exercises

1. Write about the last time you lost it. What were the outcomes, good and bad, of your rage?

2. What helps you to keep your temper? Write about what you do and how it works.

3. Who is the calmest person you know? Interview them about how they manage to take things so easy. Borrow their approach for a week; then write about the results or discuss them with a friend or colleague.

7 Try Again Later

Mañana, according to the Spanish, is the busiest day of the week. That's okay. There are times when it's best not to force things but to wait a while and try again later.

This system works like a charm when you've lost something. Think back to those times when you tore the house apart to find the missing object. If it's something important, you'll even dive into the garbage can. Still, it's never there. You begin to see red. Your life is surely ruined.

Not so fast. Relax. Try again later. You'll be surprised. The missing object is under the dish towel on the kitchen table or at the front of the filing cabinet you looked at ten times or clipped to some other paper by mistake. Or it came out of hiding all by itself just to torture you and is lying on your desk in plain view.

But don't worry. All is forgiven. The lost folder is found. The cellophane envelope with the postage stamps is just where it always was. Somehow in your haste you skipped over the delinquent object when it was there where it should have been all the time.

Or you call Mr. Jones. "Mr. Jones is in a meeting," the receptionist says. Don't hold. Don't scold. Leave him a message, or, better yet, try again later.

Good-Living Principle 7:
WISE UP by trying again later.

Optional Exercises

1. What can you do to keep from misplacing things? Write yourself some advice.

2. Do you sometimes apply the strategy of trying again later in your everyday life? Comment on the results.

3. Based on your experience, discuss the advantages and disadvantages of postponing something.

8 Take What Fits

And if it doesn't, don't! This is one of the biggest—and hardest—lessons in the book.

In the old days, spouses would keep notebooks with their partner's clothes sizes. That way they could buy their husband or wife clothes that fit

Of course, what fits goes beyond sizes. Colors, styles, and designs count too. "Yellow is a good color for you." "Blue goes well with your eyes." "That tie is too loud for you."

Quality, perceived or real, is an issue as well. "I buy Volvos and keep each for ten years." "I get a new Mercedes every three years." "A BMW is too trendy for me." "A Honda is the best I can do."

Then there are environmental concerns. "SUVs use too much fuel." "We're a one-car family." "I don't own a car. I use my bike, take public transportation, or walk."

Learn your sizes, physically and in other regards. Sometimes, as in shoes and clothes, sizes run bigger or smaller. Don't go strictly by the numbers. Try things on. Try them out. Then choose what fits.

Don't let others talk you into or out of a purchase. In the end only you can decide.

> **Good-Living Principle 8:**
> **WISE UP by taking only what fits.**

Optional Exercises

1. Write about your process for making a major purchase.

2. Have you ever been talked into buying something or making a life choice that didn't fit? Discuss the experience with a classmate or friend.

3. What have you learned about choosing a present for others or yourself? Do you do things differently now from how you did them before? How do you assess whether or not the item in question will be a good fit?

9 It's Not Always About You

> The bad plowman quarrels with his ox.
> *Korean proverb*

Don't take things to heart that don't belong there. Things others say about you are not always true. Sometimes they apply more to themselves than you.

Kids know this truth instinctively. Johnny, who is chubby, calls Freddy a "big fat rat." Freddy responds, "It takes one to know one."

Jesus made the point dramatically. People with splinters in their eye seem to criticize others for having a speck in theirs. In the kitchens of life, it seems that pots often call kettles black.

Of course, it sometimes *is* about you. You may really be overweight. In that case, get medical assistance. Slim down as best you can.

The key is to know yourself well enough to judge when criticisms of you are appropriate and should be taken seriously and when they are not. Not everything you hear is good for talk, Jamaicans say. By the same token, you shouldn't take everything seriously that others say about you.

Be critical about criticism. If what is said has merit, take it to heart and try to do better. If not, don't.

Learn to sort out which is which. Then act accordingly.

> **Good-Living Principle 9:**
> **WISE UP by learning that it's not always about you.**

Optional Exercises

1. Write about how you react to personal criticism. Do you give it back to the person? Do you take everything to heart? Do you blow it off? Are you able to sift the wheat from the chaff? Would you like to change how you react? Why?

2. How often do you criticize people? Do you do it to others? To the individuals themselves? In public or private? Do you want to change your practice? Why?

Never Say Never

> Believing something is impossible makes it so.
>
> *French proverb*

Belief can move mountains. It can also make them—from molehills. So, stay positive or at least open to the possibilities. Never say never.

Biology may or may not be destiny, as Freud alleged. Attitude, however, will surely contribute to the positive or negative outcome of our actions. Negativity is an acid that eats whatever it encounters. On the other hand, to be willing is to be able—another saying of the French.

There is the power of positive thinking. But negative thinking is powerful too. Vern McLellan has it right. Success comes in cans; failure comes in can'ts.* The choice is up to us. Say no to no by saying yes to maybe.

Some things truly are impossible, of course. You can't undress a naked person. Someone lying on the ground can't fall down. A knife can't carve its own handle. And even God can't place two mountains side by side without putting a valley between them.

Still, the range of what can be done is huge and growing. Yesterday's impossibilities are today's realities. "They'll never put a man on the moon!" Well? "Beam me up, Scotty." Don't count it out.

> **Good-Living Principle 10:**
> **WISE UP by never saying never.**

Optional Exercises

1. Did you ever think something was impossible that you were later able to do? Write about it.

2. Who is the most positive person you know? What is their life like?

3. Is there something you are trying to do now that could profit from an attitude adjustment? Share about it with a friend.

*Vern McLellan, *The Complete Book of Practical Proverbs & Wacky Wit* (Wheaton, Illinois: Tyndale House Publishers, Inc., 1996), p. 70.

Little by Little

Grain by grain,
a loaf—stone by
stone, a castle.
Yugoslav proverb

We Americans are sprinters, not distance runners. In the Olympics we do best in shorter events. We also like to do things now, get them done, and win big. Patience is not an American virtue.

Yet most achievements—a good wine or a beautiful building—take time. Rushing can mess things up. In working math problems, for example, it's best to proceed step by step. Even good students make mistakes by skipping steps.

When Aesops' tortoise and hare race, remember who wins. Slow and steady takes the day. We avoid this ancient wisdom at our peril.

Twelve Step Programs urge their members to move forward "one day at a time." It makes the process of recovery from addiction doable.

Hit the pitch you are thrown. Not the last pitch. Not the pitch you think you're getting. Stick to the business at hand and meet the ball where it is.

Little by little gets books written, houses built, debts paid, mountains climbed, and trust funds established. Little by little develops solid businesses and good relationships too. This ancient secret is still relevant today.

> **Good-Living Principle 11:**
> **WISE UP by doing things incrementally.**

Optional Exercises

1. Have you ever accomplished something by following the principle of little by little? What was the outcome? Write about it for class, journal on it, or share your reflections with a friend.

2. What is your longest friendship to date? How have you managed to keep it fresh and solid?

3. Did you ever mess something up by trying to get it done too fast? Describe the situation, what lessons you took from it, and how you might act differently if faced with a similar situation in future.

Attend to the Details

There are big-picture people and detail people. To do well in life, you need to be something of both.

Good ideas are important. Without them nothing valuable would ever get done. But ideas alone are not enough. They have to massaged, worked out, refined. They need to be vetted, weighed, assessed. The devil's in the details.

The Germans have a saying, "Becoming a parent isn't that tough. Being a parent is where things get rough." (*Eltern Werden ist nicht schwer; Eltern Sein dagegen sehr.*) You have to attend to the small change of parenthood: Listen to your kids. Be patient. Remain pleasant. And do all this with consistency during the long years of school meetings, Scouts, band concerts, and soccer games.

The idea of having children is one thing. Actually having them, then being peaceful, effective parents is something else. Impatience with one's children can lead to abuse. The devil is definitely in the details.

Projects need to be well-thought-out, carefully planned, and attentively carried out. I's must be dotted and T's crossed. Try skipping over the details and they will trip you up.

God may be in the great ideas, but the devil is always in the details.

Good-Living Principle 12:
WISE UP by attending to the details.

Optional Exercises

1. Think about the biggest project you ever managed. What was it, and how did it turn out? Speak with a friend about how well you attended to the details.

2. If you were to undertake this project again, what would you do differently? Why?

3. Who is the most detail-oriented person you know? Write about her or him. What are the plusses and minuses of giving so much attention to details?

Get the Big Picture

If the devil is in the details, God is in the big picture. Don't get bogged down in minutia. Don't miss the forest for the trees.

Details are important, of course. But you can waste your whole life hanging out with the wrong people, living in the wrong place, working at the wrong profession, and barking up the wrong tree. These are big-picture concerns.

It's better to do the right thing fairly well than the wrong thing perfectly. Get the big picture first, since a little attention to something beats much ado about nothing.

Some bosses nickel-and-dime their workers by correcting small mistakes while never commenting on the job as a whole. They never take the time to praise those things that were well-done. They forget about the importance of building up good relations with their work team.

You can take the edge off a good job with a small mistake. But even if you handle all the small points well, that will never make up for something done without enthusiasm or understanding.

Leaders do right things, managers do things right. Managers focus on details, leaders on the big picture. Details, to be sure, are important, but the big picture must come first. Forget it at your peril.

> **Good-Living Principle 13:**
> **WISE UP by getting the big picture.**

Optional Exercises

1. Write about how well you track the big picture throughout planning and implementing a project.

2. Have you ever gotten bogged down in details? Talk with a friend about the situation and how you resolved it.

3. Share how the best leader you know keeps his helpers focused on the grand scheme as they work together on something.

14 Watch Out

> The crab that walks too far falls into the pot.
>
> *Haitian Proverb*

Most of the world's proverbs advise caution. Life is a minefield, so watch your step.

We Americans as a group are a trusting lot. Europeans, who have lived through too many wars on their soil, think we are naïve. Maybe they are right. But things have changed since 9/11.

In the old days—before 9/11—if we worried at all, we would quote Leroy "Satchel" Paige, the African American baseball great. "Don't look back," Satchel said. "Something may be gaining on you." Nowadays we look back all the time and wonder if a vacation at home might not be better than a plane trip anywhere.

It's a shame to have to add this advice to our recipe for good living in the new century. Unfortunately, that's just how things are. Life has always been risky. So, until there's a basic change in how we humans act toward one another, it's foolish to throw caution to the winds.

Be nice, pleasant, and hospitable, but remember. Be careful with strangers. They may have more than feet in their shoes. Get to know the people you deal with, and entrust important matters only to those you know well.

Charity begins at home, and in the present era this is especially true in human relations. All in all, you're best advised to be careful.

Good-Living Principle 14: WISE UP by watching out.

Optional Exercises

1. Write about a time when you weren't vigilant enough and paid the price.

2. Journal about someone who is overly cautious, even by today's standards.

3. If you were to counsel a younger friend on how to be careful in a balanced way, what advice would you give?

Celebrate Commonalities

You are in a foreign country. Suddenly someone is speaking your language. Or you see a billboard advertising a familiar product. Or you spot a chain restaurant from home. Blessed are the ties that bind.

You run into to an elementary-school friend at the mall. Being with her reminds you of all the fun you had playing "in the good old days" before the pressures of high school. Blessed are the ties that bind.

You go to a family reunion. Your relatives come from all over the country. Some you haven't seen for years. Yet you have that familiar feeling even with them. Blessed are the ties that bind.

You go to an all-state band concert. You have been playing clarinet since 5th grade. You see the boy, now a young man, who played next to you until his family moved away in eighth grade. As you eat lunch together, you reminisce about all the silly things you'd do during rehearsal. Blessed are the ties that bind.

Commonalities are the comfort food of living. Being from the same place, generation, or family gives us a sense of familiarity, of home. So does shared experience. Life is full of dislocation and change. Blessed are the ties that bind.

> **Good-Living Principle 15:**
> **WISE UP by celebrating commonalities.**

Optional Exercises

1. Write about an experience where you felt alone until something unexpectedly reminded you of home.

2. What common bonds give you the greatest sense of comfort? Respond in an essay or share thoughts with a classmate or friend.

3. In a letter, thank someone for the things they do that support you in your daily living. Mail the letter if you wish.

16 Celebrate Difference

Variety is the spice of life. Think how boring it would be to eat the same food, wear the same clothes, or do the same things every day. Three cheers for Thai restaurants and vacations. For exercise and naps. For new people in our lives.

An Austrian couple we know thank the Universe every New Year's Eve for the interesting new people they will meet in the year ahead. New people and new experiences. New possibilities. Change may be frightening, but variety is good.

There is a great divide among people. One group thinks difference is bad. Never trust a stranger. People who wear funny clothes or speak with an accent are to be avoided. You can never tell what they are thinking. Difference is bad, even dangerous.

Another group thinks difference is good. How can you learn if everyone thinks the same thoughts or likes the same things? Two heads are better than one for that very reason. Two people can pool their thoughts, share their insights, and come up with something better than what either alone might achieve.

Of course, not all difference is good. The earth is either flat or round. The two ideas are not equally valid. Still, in general, difference is good. We can be happy that our diverse world is growing smaller.

Good-Living Principle 16:
WISE UP by celebrating difference.

Optional Exercises

1. Journal about a situation where some difference opened you to a new way of thinking or acting.

2. Are there people or circumstances in your life so different that you find them hard to accept? Write how you might deal with them more effectively.

3. Share about the most distinctive person you know. What have you learned by associating with this individual?

17 Respect Yourself

This principle is basic. Yet like most basic things, it's hard. First of all, you have to start further back than Shakespeare. In the 5th Century BCE, Socrates was advised by the Oracle of Delphi to "know thyself." In other words, you can't be true to yourself until you know who you are.

So who is this person I call me? How can I get to know who I really am?

Start by asking yourself these questions. What do I like and dislike? What comes easy to me and what is hard? What are my dreams? What makes me happy or sad?

By answering honestly, you will begin to know yourself better.

Then, you respect that person by being (or becoming) him or her as deeply and consistently as possible.

Say you love the outdoors. But another person convinces you to

become a lawyer because you are
smart and can speak well in front
of people. Also, lawyers make lots
of money. Yet what's the point of
choosing a profession that keeps you
indoors? Maybe you should be a forest
ranger, a gardener, a cowboy.

Respect yourself by knowing who you
are and acting accordingly. It's hard to
be happy doing anything else.

Good-Living Principle 17:
WISE UP by respecting yourself.

Optional Exercises

1. Write an essay or journal entry in
   which you describe who you are
   in terms of basic likes and dislikes,
   what comes easy to you or hard,
   and what makes you happy or sad.

2. Describe the behavior of someone
   who disrespects himself or herself.

3. Share about someone you know
   who most fully embodies Polonius's
   advice to his son: "To thine own self
   be true...."

18 Respect Others

Gold is found in many countries. So it is not surprising that sayings like the Golden Rule of Christianity—Do unto others as you would have others do unto you—are found in other religions as well.

To be accurate, some religions have a Silver, or negative Golden, Rule. Confucianism, Judaism, and Buddhism all advise that you should not do things to others that you wouldn't want others doing to you. In short, refrain from doing bad. Good will be the result.

But if you really want to do right by others, you have to go beyond the Silver and Golden Rules and aspire to follow the Platinum. After all, people differ. Your meat may be my poison.

For example, penicillin may have saved your life. But your friend is deathly allergic to it. If she comes

down with a dangerous infection
and you inject her with penicillin, she
may die of penicillin shock despite your
good intentions.

Respecting others means giving them
space to be themselves. The Golden Rule
may work in most cases. But be careful.
You never know when it won't. So it's
best to switch to a higher standard. From
now on, practice the Platinum Rule.

**Good-Living Principle 18:
WISE UP by respecting others.**

Optional Exercises

1. How are you at giving people the space
   they need to be themselves? Respond
   to this question in your journal.

2. Write a set of "ten commandments"
   on how you'd like others to treat you.

3. Who respects you the least? Write a
   private journal essay in which you
   give yourself some advice on how to
   get that person to treat you with
   more respect.

The Power of One

19

> A man with God is always in the majority.
>
> *John Knox,*
> *16th Century*

The three Abrahamic faiths—Judaism, Christianity, and Islam—agree that God is one. Their emphases, however, differ.

For Judaism God is One. For Christianity, One but in three Persons. For Islam, One and Only—there being no other god but God, *the* God, which is what Allah literally means. Even Hinduism, known for polytheism, states that beyond the many gods there is only One, called Brahman.

The Power of One is important. Think of a simple atom. When it is split, incredible power is released. Yet that's the power of fragmentation, fission. Much greater power comes from fusing elements into a single new atom like hydrogen. Even in nature, the power of one trumps the power of many.

That's why it's important to rev up your personal power by getting your act together. Consolidate your bills. Even clean up your room. Carl Jung, the psychiatrist, helped his patients get well by re-integrating themselves psychologically. Integration leads to integrity. Disintegration to duplicity.

As you work on yourself, you become a whole person. Whole and holy are related words and concepts in English. Saints are simply people who have gotten their acts together and have used their personal power for the greater good. What about you?

Good-Living Principle 19: WISE UP by realizing the Power of One.

Optional Exercises

1. Who is the most "together" person you know? Write about him or her in your journal or for a class assignment.

2. What are you doing to develop yourself into a more integrated, less fragmented human being? Discuss this question with a friend or write about it in your journal.

3. What are your biggest barriers to personal development? Journal about them.

The Power of Many

We may be back to the Power of One. Many working together generate strength. Ten arrows are easily broken, one at a time. Only when bundled together do they become unbreakable.

The Power of Many can be seen in other areas too. Think of the miracle of regular savings. A financial planning book for youth says if you save $5 a week from age 25, you'll be a millionaire on your 65th birthday. Of course, you can't skip a week or take anything out. Also, this calculation is based on compound interest of three or four percent. Still, the lesson is clear. Small amounts saved regularly can lead to great wealth.

The environmental movement makes the same point. If one person in a materially developed country lives lightly on the earth, the effect is trivial. But if the whole population starts doing so, the effect is transformative.

The Power of Many is clear in society too. Think of the American Civil
Rights Movement. A few courageous
leaders and organizations were able to
spark the resistance of the majority
of African Americans. Soon other
ethnic groups joined in, and laws
began to change.

Participate in the Power of Many by
joining a social-action group or regularly feeding a savings plan.

Good-Living Principle 20:
WISE UP by using the Power of Many.

Optional Exercises

1. Journal on another example of the
   Power of Many.

2. Write about a leader able to get a
   group of people to work successfully for a common goal. What makes
   this individual so effective?

3. Discuss with a friend how you
   intend to use the Power of Many
   in the next six months.

21 Don't Worry

> There are
> two days…
> about which….
> I never worry…
> Yesterday…
> and…Tomorrow.
>
> *Robert Jones
> Burdette, d. 1914*

"Don't worry." It's easier said than done. Still, worrying is like revving your car on ice. You don't get anywhere. You only burn your treads and dig yourself into a deeper rut.

What's done can't be undone. "The rice has become porridge," say the Indonesians. "You can't take the cream back from the coffee," say the Haitians. And we Anglo-Americans add, "There's no use crying over spilled milk."

In other words, you should eat the porridge, drink the coffee, and—before someone slips on the floor—clean up the spilled milk. In short, you should make the best of your situation and get on with living.

What about the future? Anything could happen. We could even die. Could? We will die. But worrying about death distracts us from our main job of living. And living has one salient feature: It happens only in the present.

If we're busy worrying about past or future, we can't pay attention to the present. We are unavailable to smell the roses.

Not worrying is hard. But the habit is a weed that chokes the flowers and fruits of living. So remember: The past is history, the future's a mystery, and the present's a gift, just as the name says. Stop worrying. Start living

---

Good-Living Principle 21:
WISE UP by not worrying.

Optional Exercises

1. Write about when and how you worry. What conclusions do you draw?

2. Brainstorm with a friend about techniques to avoid worry.

3. Think about a time when you seemed to be most worry-free. How might you re-create that time today?

Be Happy

22

> Don't worry!
> Be happy!
> *Bobby McFarrin's song title*

If there is anything harder than not worrying, it's probably being happy. Still, the two go together, generally in that order.

Now, you may think telling someone to "be happy" is the dumbest piece of advice in this book. We all want to be happy. Yet you can't just be happy on command. It's like trying to tickle yourself. Plus doesn't genetics have something to do with it? Aren't there people with happy-go-lucky dispositions while others seem hardwired for depression, bitterness, or anger?

Yes and no. Some people clearly seem born to happiness. Even in the worst situations, they find something to laugh about. But you'd be surprised how you can cheer yourself up. Aerobic exercise, for example, gets those endorphins flowing. They are nature's anti-depressant. Or take Zorba the Greek's advice and go dancing.

Another technique is doing something helpful for others. Visiting a shut-in or driving a senior to a medical appointment comes to mind. Or asking a teenager about life and listening without interrupting for five minutes.

Completing a chore is another tonic, if not for happiness, at least for lightening things up. That's step one. Cultivating happiness means doing things you like, seeking out people that make you laugh, and being grateful for everything. Above all, avoid stress. Remember: Don't worry. Be happy.

Good-Living Principle 22:
WISE UP by being happy.

Optional Exercises

1. When was the last time you were really happy? Reflect about that time including what you think the causes of your happiness were.

2. Interview the happiest person you know. Ask how they keep from getting sad.

3. Try some technique to cheer yourself up. Then journal about the results.

23 Seize the Day

> Eat, drink, and make merry, for tomorrow we die.
> *See Luke 12:19-20*

How hedonistic! How depressing! If we are all doomed, shouldn't we at least be serious and take care of business?

Okay. Have it your way. "Work, work, work, for tomorrow we die." Like that any better?

Take your choice of epitaphs. "Here lies Jane Doe. She played herself to death." Or: "Here lies Jane Doe. She worked herself to death."

One thing is clear. Our limited time means every day should count. A World-War-II-era song puts it succinctly" "Enjoy yourself. / It's later than you think. / . . . The time goes by as quickly as a wink. / So enjoy yourself, enjoy yourself. / It's later than you think."

Balance, of course, is the main caution. All work and no play makes Jack a dull boy. And Jill a dull girl.

So seize the day but don't strangle it. Balance work with play and play with work. In fact, make your work playful and your play meaningful. Even silly play has its place, like holes in Swiss cheese.

Robert Frost, the American poet, said you're living rightly "when work is play for mortal stakes." It's work. It's fun. But it also counts.

Or, to borrow Studs Terkel's tagline, "Take it easy, but take it."

Tomorrow we may die, but as for today, we're living.

Good-Living Principle 23:
WISE UP by living each day to the fullest.

Optional Exercises

1. How do you balance work with play? Do you go to extremes? Can you moderate? Discuss these questions in your journal.

2. Write about a typical day. What changes would you like to make? Why?

3. Who's the most playful person you know? Journal about him or her.

24 Plan

> It's not the man,
> it's the plan.
> It's not the rap,
> it's the map.
> *Ossie Davis*

Spontaneity has its place. But accomplishing something of value usually requires planning.

Giving a talk? Better think about what you want to say and how you'll say it. Who's your audience? You talk one way about Shakespeare to 8th graders and another to graduate students in English.

Now all this may sound obvious. But many a professor has puzzled college freshmen by teaching as if to grad students. Think about such questions beforehand. Decide on a strategy. Then go for it.

Plan your vacations too. You can always make changes later. Yet a fully unplanned trip may find you wiring home for money, if, that is, you have a home to wire to or folks there who can come through.

Think about the sorts of things you'd like to do in life and go after the knowledge and skills you'll most likely need to be able to do them. Interview people who are already doing what you'd like to do. Ask them their advice on how best to prepare. Reflect critically on what they tell you. Let some time go by. Then make your plans.

Plans, like bylaws and constitutions, can always be amended. They are the proverbial stake in the ground. But you can't amend what you've never created. So take a tip from champion chess players—or NASA. Plan. Plan. Plan.

Good-Living Principle 24:
WISE UP by making plans.

Optional Exercises

1. Think about something you did without planning that really went wrong. What lessons can you draw?

2. Not every plan works. Journal about one you had to revise or drop.

3. Write yourself some tips on effective planning. What's your main conclusion?

25 Read

> The man [!] who doesn't read good books has no advantage over the man who can't read them.
>
> *Mark Twain*

Being literate is only half the battle. In this day of 999 TV channels, reading may be an endangered activity. Thank goodness for airplane travel. You still see a proliferation there of fat paperbacks. Popular works for the most part, but at least you see books.

Yet books are only half the battle. There are classics and literary fast food. The easy read and the page-turner have their place. But if that's all there is, per Peggy Lee, you'd better keep dancing.

It's essential to experience the pleasure of hanging out with the great people of yesterday and today. Jung, Mother Teresa, Nelson Mandela, Rigoberta Menchu, the Dalai Lama, Gandhi, Viktor Frankl, Einstein, Helen Keller. The list goes on. Make up your own.

Don't forget the great poets, play-wrights, and novelists—individuals who've done incredible things with words. Even translations—from the Classics of China and India to the Greek epics and tragedies, Roman poetry, Dante, Goethe, the great Russian and French novelists—should be read despite the loss of the original language. Such works provide insight into different times, places, cultures, and lives. TV is good at this too. But TV spells it all out. Get a good book. Read. Then imagine yourself into the hearts and minds of others.

**Good-Living Principle 25:
WISE UP by reading good books.**

Optional Exercises

1. What was the best book you ever read? Journal about it.

2. Interview someone you regard highly. Ask them for the title of their favorite book. Read it; then discuss it with them.

3. Go shopping with a friend, buy a short book, and read it out loud to each other.

26 Travel

Take your show on the road, and the road will show you the world. Not that you can't learn at home. But Des Moines isn't Paris. And Paris isn't Casablanca. And Casablanca isn't Bombay. And Bombay isn't the Golden Road to Samarkand.

By going away to a really different place, you'll learn who you are. And what home is. And how not everything in that new place is all that different. And how not everything back home is necessarily better.

Each of us studied in a foreign country as a young adult. At 19 Reynold went to Heidelberg, Germany, as a junior-year exchange student. Yale students had been spending two semesters at Heidelberg University for years. But as a Jewish-American student thirteen years after World War II, Reynold had a special experience.

At 20 Jan came to America from Dhaka, the capital of Bangladesh, not far from the Indian city of Calcutta. A Muslim, he studied at a small Christian college, Berea, in rural Kentucky.

In both cases, our lives were changed forever. We saw things that were new, different, even startling. But mainly, we met people who valued us for ourselves. We learned first hand that, though individuals differ, humanity is one

Home is our nest, but our habitat is the sky. We need to seek out new worlds and learn the unity of creation. There's only one way to do this. Travel.

> **Good-Living Principle 26:**
> **WISE UP by traveling.**

Optional Exercises

1. Journal about the best trip you ever took. What made it so special?

2. Write briefly on the most important learning thus far from your travels.

3. Discuss with a friend or colleague where you'd like to travel next.

27 Trust Your Instincts

If you have a strong feeling about
something, go with it. Especially if
you keep pushing that feeling away,
and it keeps coming back. Your
instruments are telling you something. Trust them.

Where decisions have a lot riding on
them—operate, don't operate; buy
the land, don't—we all tend to be
cautious. A bad judgment call could
mean bankruptcy or worse. Better
think things over. Get a second, third,
even fourth opinion. Sleep on it.
Then sleep on it some more.

Still, we don't always have the luxury
of time to reach our verdicts. Life
sometimes requires us to decide and
move on. What then?

Trust your instincts.

Okay, you protest, but there are
times when the impulses driving me
may not represent my highest self.
Well, if that's the case and you know

it, you are already ahead of the game. Usually, strong passions are urgent, intense, and short-lived. Let them pass.

Your intuition, by contrast, is typically a still, small voice which keeps coming back. Dismiss the passions, but trust your instincts. They are your guidance system—like that which conducts birds thousands of miles each year to their winter home.

Critics, even friends and colleagues, may offer advice. At the end of the day, take what you like, leave the rest, and go with your gut.

Good-Living Principle 27:
WISE UP by trusting your instincts.

Optional Exercises

1. Journal on how do you distinguish your intuition from your passions.

2. Do you always march to your own drummer, or do you tend to follow others' advice? Write about how balanced you are in this regard.

3. Ask the most intuitive person you know for tips on trusting one's instincts.

Wising UP 81

28 Live

> May you live
> all the days
> of your life.
> *Jonathan Swift*

Where there's life, there's hope.
Mere breathing doesn't do it. Eating,
sleeping, and walking around don't
either. Life is more than going
through the motions. Showing up
is only half of living.

In other words, life is an opportunity.
The Universe's part, so to speak, is to
provide us this chance. Our part is to
make something of it.

We are given a life but earn a living.
There is no free lunch. But this is really
good news. Life urges us to learn the
inner game of living, to live from the
inside out, from our essence and talents, not our personality or mask.

We can be inert, unmoving, like a thing.
We can have a heart like a stone. We
can be a vegetable, attached to a
machine, barely breathing. We can
be an animal, fighting anyone who
threatens our territory. We can be all
too human—fallible, not keeping our
promises, turning away.

Or we can be a developing, growing human being, a little lower than the angels and acting that way. Not a robot. Not a Goody Two-Shoes. But someone who lives up to the promise of feet-on-the-ground and head-in-the-stars. The child of Mother Earth and Father Sky—strong, humble, filled with spirit. Showing a family resemblance.

Life must be lived. It's not a spectator sport.

Good-Living Principle 28:
WISE UP by really living your life.

Optional Exercises

1. What are you doing each day to live the best life you can? Discuss this question with a classmate or friend.

2. Write about a time when you were sleep-walking through life. What was it like?

3. Journal on the "most alive" person you know. How does s/he live their life?

Have Faith

> The strength
> of the heart
> comes from the
> soundness of
> the faith.
> *Arabic saying*

Faith is a gift. Christians use the terms grace or blessing. The Javanese of Indonesia, mainly Muslims, say *anugraha*—something of great value which comes from beyond your expectations or deserts.

So if faith is a gift, how can someone tell you to have it? No problem. Kids do this all the time. They ask their parents for a bike at Christmas, a stereo for their birthday, a series of DVDs for Hanukkah, a new leather outfit for Id, their own TV for Buddha's Birthday.

The Christian formula is **A.S.K. Ask** and you will receive. **Seek** and you will find. **Knock** and the door will be opened. That's the order in the Bible. The initiation, though, has to come from you.

What if you don't believe in God? A lot of people don't. Anyone with eyes can find thousands of arguments against an all-good, all-powerful deity concerned for the well-being of the planet. Yet there are counterarguments too. "Blessed is the moon," say the Samoans. "It goes away but it comes back."

The important thing (initially) is to have faith in yourself, life, regularity, and possibility. Where there's life, there's hope. If God exists, as the two of us believe, God will reach down to all hands reaching up, including yours.

Meanwhile, have faith.

> **Good-Living Principle 29:**
> **WISE UP by having faith.**

Optional Exercises

1. Do you believe in God? Why? Why not? Would you like to? Why? Why not? Respond to these questions in the privacy of your journal.

2. Who is your role model for faith? Discuss that person with a friend or classmate.

3. Write an essay on what helps you have or keeps you from having faith.

30 Remember to Doubt

> To believe with certainty, we must begin by doubting.
>
> *Polish proverb*

Confidence games depend on the victim's believing everything.

Even seeing isn't always believing. From the perspective of the highest mountain, the earth still looks flat. It took a leap to declare it round. Not till space travel—or supersonic flight—could we confirm this reality with our senses.

The scientific method is based on doubting. Skepticism is an old gift of the human race, based most likely on hard experience. Uncle Uthgar ate the wrong mushroom. Whoops! Better avoid that kind in future.

Once burnt, twice shy. In fact, most of the world's proverbs are cautionary. Look before you leap. If you call one wolf, you invite the pack (Bulgarian). Though honey is sweet, don't lick it off a briar. (Irish) And so on.

The ancient Greeks never forgot the Trojan horse, a ruse that led to the fall of Troy. "Remember to distrust" became a favorite saying of theirs.

Of course, if you doubted everything, your life would be short. Fearing that all your food was poisoned, you'd starve yourself to death. But a little healthy distrust is a good preventive. Don't open the door to everyone. Know who you're talking to. Reveal only as much as necessary. The Poles also say, "The person who is always nice is not always nice."

So, remember to doubt. Einstein did— and he changed the world.

> **Good-Living Principle 30:**
> **WISE UP by applying healthy skepticism.**

Optional Exercises

1. Do you tend to believe too much or too little? Journal about how you balance trust with skepticism.

2. Who's your role model for healthy skepticism? Do an oral report on him or her.

3. Write about a case where the scientific method was effectively applied.

31 Move It or Lose It

Sometimes it seems like we are standing in a traffic intersection, waiting for the light to change. Paralysis takes over, and we are helpless. Even though we are awake, we can't seem to wake up.

It's time to encourage ourselves: Move it or lose it!

An old trick is to hit yourself lightly on your head, neck, chest, and torso. Somehow this procedure stimulates the blood flow and has the effect of caffeine without the side effects. Of course, you may not want to resort to this technique in public—in a busy intersection, say. But you'll be surprised how effective this little self-maintenance trick is.

Another technique is simply to start. If you have a big job to do, don't let the size daunt you. Even the highest mountain gets climbed the same way, one step at a time. The hardest part is getting started. Most Western languages have a proverb illustrating the point. "Every beginning is difficult" is how both the Germans and the Italians put it. (*Jeder Anfang ist schwer,* and *Ogni principio è dificile.*) We English speakers say, "Well begun is half done."

The "or lose it" part has to do with the sad truth that if we wait too long to do something, the opportunity may evaporate.

So, wake up, get started, seize the day. The shortest delay may lose us the game.

Good-Living Principle 31:
WISE UP by getting started.

Optional Exercises

1. Write about your work habits. How are you at moving projects along? What tends to bog you down?

2. Write yourself a letter containing five pieces of advice to get yourself going.

3. Share time-management techniques with a friend over coffee.

32 Take Your Time

32

> You can't out-run the devil—only outwait him. *original proverb*

Is there any skill harder—or more necessary—than patience? Most of the world's folk wisdom makes this point: Slow and steady wins the race. Measure ten times, cut once. And a personal favorite, from Africa, which spices patience with discretion: Don't call the alligator big-mouth till after you've crossed the river.

Wait till you're there. Strike when the iron is hot. All things come in due season. The foolish farmer, the Chinese say, tries to make the rice grow faster by pulling on the shoot.

Chinese philosophy takes this concept to its logical conclusion in Taoism—the study of the Way (Tao) and its power. The sage, says Lao Tsu, governs the kingdom without ever leaving home. The one who achieves the most does the least. The Chinese characters—pronounced *oo* and *way* in Mandarin—literally mean "Don't do."

Economy of effort seems the lesson. In English we say, "All things come to those who wait."

Watch a cat hunt. She finds a hiding place and waits for prey. She waits and waits and waits. Then, at just the right time, she springs. Sometimes the prey gets away. Usually it doesn't.

Cats are successful hunters because they take their time. They wait till the situation is just right and then do what they have to. Take a lesson from them and learn to do the same.

> **Good-Living Principle 32:**
> **WISE UP by taking your time.**

Optional Exercises

1. How patient are you? Write about your conclusions in your journal.

2. How might you become more patient? Write yourself a letter with some advice.

3. Can you really achieve more by doing less? Discuss this idea with a friend or colleague.

Just Say "Thank You"

> When eating a fruit, think of the person who planted the tree.
> *Vietnamese proverb*

"Please is hot, thanks are cold," say the Germans. It's true. When you need something, you plan and work and cajole to get it. Once you have it, though, it takes an effort to say "thank you."

We human beings take a lot for granted. The sun always rises. The moon goes away but comes back. The heart in a 70-year-old person has already beaten two billion times. Yet, when was the last time we thanked the sun? The moon? Our heart?

Deprivation is a good reminder. When the New England Puritans were starving during their first winter, the local Native tribe sent them food. The Puritans thanked God—and, let's hope, their neighbors—for saving them. (Later, the Native peoples of the United States were thanked in general by being pushed off ancestral lands by their European guests.)

People who survive wars, vehicle crashes, and major surgery are also grateful. Too bad it takes such experiences to remind us of the fragility of life and how dependent we are on others and Nature.

When children are complimented, they generally don't know what to do. Littler ones sometimes run away. Parents coach their kids to "just say thank you." We should take this lesson into adulthood by being grateful for everything. Who knows? Today's setback may lead to tomorrow's triumph.

> **Good-Living Principle 33:**
> **WISE UP by being grateful.**

Optional Exercises

1. If you pray regularly for things, spend a week thanking the Universe instead for what you have received. Then journal about the experience.

2. Write about someone you know who seems grateful despite misfortune.

3. How do you handle compliments? Discuss this topic with a classmate or friend.

34 Listen

> Having two ears and one tongue, we should listen twice as much as we speak.
>
> *Turkish proverb*

What a tall order—especially for extroverts! The pressure to control the world by talking is often irresistible.

Introverts have an easier time. For them, talking is the challenge. They live by the gold standard: Speaking is silver; silence, golden.

Today's principle is directed to the talkers of the world—those with more tongues than ears. Learn to think of others as persons living in your head. Let them speak. Like your inner voices, they may have something worth hearing.

Just as other people can scratch your back in the places you can't reach, others may see things you can't see. Listen and learn.

Don't interrupt. Let them finish their thoughts. Don't think about what you want to say next. When the time comes, if you have something to say, you'll say it. If you forget, either it wasn't important or you'll remember it later. If something goes without saying, it goes without saying.

Twelve Step Program participants are trained to listen. The unwritten rule in these groups is "never interrupt." Individual sharing is generally limited to a few minutes, and most people comply. Still, there are times when an individual needs to speak longer. Then, force yourself to listen. There may be a blessing in it for everyone.

> **Good-Living Principle 34:**
> **WISE UP by listening more than you speak.**

Optional Exercises

1. Are you a listener or a talker? Discuss with a friend or classmate where the two of you fall on the talker-listener spectrum.

2. Go on a talking fast—or listening fiesta—for a day. Journal about the experience and what you learned.

3. Interview someone who is a good listener. Write about their approach.

35 Speak Up

If you have
something
to say, say it.
American proverb

This tip is directed to introverts—those who would rather die than speak. Congratulations on your silence, especially if you are actively listening to others. You have chosen the better part.

Still, there are times when you need to speak up. In such instances, keeping your peace is wrong. If you have something to say, say it.

But what if the other person doesn't like what you say? What if what you say is foolish or embarrassing?

You can always preface your statements with phrases like "in my view" or "based on my experience." After all, everyone is entitled to an opinion. As long as you don't put the other person down—even if you think they're totally off base—you'll be fine. Learning to disagree without being disagreeable is one of life's fine arts. Who knows? By speaking your piece, you may be helping another person modify or moderate their opinion.

Of course, practice makes perfect. So, try your ideas out first with people who feel safe. As you gain confidence, move on to acquaintances and eventually strangers.

Speaking in public is said to be our greatest fear after the fear of death. No wonder comics talk about "dying out there." But if you've got something to say, say it. Your words might mean the difference between life and death for someone else.

Good-Living Principle 35:
WISE UP by speaking your mind.

Optional Exercises

1. If you find it hard to speak with others or in groups, meet with a trusted friend and ask advice.

2. Find a role model, note down some of their words and phrases, and borrow them.

3. Journal periodically on the progress you are making in speaking out.

36 Stay Calm

In the U.S. we have a number of expressions for panicking: *Going ape, going bananas, freaking out, wigging out, going crazy, going nuts, going around the bend,* and *bonkers* are examples. Readers will doubtless think of others.

Probably the reason for this abundance is that we do it so much. Panicking may be as common for most of us as getting angry. Some people even seem to pride themselves on how often they wig out. "Man, I just go nuts!" They'll say. It's almost like a personal characteristic. "My hair is blond, my eyes are blue, and I freak out all the time."

Can't you see the personal ad in the newspaper? "White European-American male, 38, five-foot-ten, 165 pounds, non-smoker, likes to freak out. Seeking partner with similar interest."

Of course, deep inside, many of us look up to, even envy, the John Waynes of the world—the cool, quiet types who go about their business in the midst of the storm.

New York City's ex-mayor, Rudy Giuliani, used to be considered a hothead. Because of his performance during 9-11, he's now become America's new John Wayne. When asked how he managed to stay calm in the midst of the Trade Tower disaster, he said he'd followed his father's advice: the bigger the crisis, the calmer you should become.

In a difficult situation, keeping your cool may get you through.

Good-Living Principle 36: WISE UP by staying calm.

Optional Exercises

1. Write about an extreme situation you once experienced and how you dealt with it.

2. If you were to re-live that situation, would you react differently? Why?

3. Do you have a role model for keeping their cool? Write about her or him.

37 Follow the Rules

> Those not ruled by the rudder will be ruled by the rocks.
>
> *Welsh saying*

One of the gifts of modern society is the traffic light. By telling drivers when to stop or go, it regulates traffic and gives everyone their chance. Running a red light is dangerous. The consequences are sometimes fatal.

Rules, if they are fair, keep us from hurting or killing each other. They ensure a measure of justice. You get yours. I get mine. Society gets its. Rules, whether in a game or life, keep the playing field level. They guarantee that opportunities will be roughly even and that give-and-take prevails.

Both of us authors have lived in places where traffic lights are not so prevalent. Where a short taxi ride can feel like a trip to the moon. No wonder people in less-developed countries have so much faith. They need it!

Rules are the basis for order. Nature itself runs on them. Can you imagine the consequences if the world stopped spinning, the moon rising, or the sun shining? The ecology movement's main goal is to help us live in harmony with Nature's rules.

Human rules sometimes drive us crazy. They are not always fair or may have unintended consequences. That's why in democracies constitutions can be amended, laws rescinded, and new laws enacted. In the end, though, rules make society possible.

> **Good-Living Principle 37:**
> **WISE UP by following the rules.**

Optional Exercises

1. Do you jay-walk, exceed speed limits, occasionally run red lights? In your journal write yourself a letter on what behaviors to change and why.

2. Review your eating and drinking habits. How might you better rule your body?

3. Write a paragraph on the meaning of the Welsh proverb on the opposite page.

38 Go Outside the Box

> People who do not break things first will never learn to create anything.
>
> *Filipino saying*

Rules are great, except when it comes to creativity. If our ancestors had followed the way things were always done, nothing would ever have changed.

Think about it. If Columbus had submitted to the truth of his day that the earth was flat, the new world would have remained undiscovered. If Galileo had accepted the apparent fact that the sun circled the earth, we'd still be thinking geocentrically. Or if Picasso, Kandinsky, and others had agreed that painters should show reality like a camera, abstract art and its joys would never have been invented.

Cultures are self-contained boxes. They are like tiny spaces where cats can curl up and feel supported. They have their place and are not to be disdained.

On the other hand, creativity is all about breaking the rules and going outside the boxes of conventional seeing, feeling, and doing. It's about new, unconventional ways to solve problems. Craziness, it's said, is doing the same thing over and over and expecting different results.

Entrepreneurs attend seminars on innovation and outside-the-box thinking. Who, after all, would inject poison into themselves or friends? It goes totally against logic and ethics. Yet that kind of thinking led to vaccines against dread diseases, antidotes to snakebite, and chemotherapy. So, when it comes to creativity, forget about the rules.

> **Good-Living Principle 38:**
> **WISE UP by going outside the box.**

Optional Exercises

1. Are you a conventional thinker or an innovator? Discuss this question in your journal. Would you like to change? How and why?

2. Share with someone else how you solved a problem by going outside the box.

3. Write a one-page essay on the most creative person you know.

Know Yourself

39

> ## Know thyself!
> *The Delphic Oracle's advice to Socrates*

This is where it all begins, with knowing who you really are. You can't drive a car or fly a plane without knowing how. You can't read a book without understanding the language. You can't operate a washing machine or a computer without following the instructions. So how in the world can you be you without knowing who you are and how you work?

You can of course go through the motions. The results will be humorous at best and ruinous to yourself and others at worst.

Without learning who you are, you will be a square peg for round holes. You will study a major for which you have little interest and take jobs which don't draw on your main talents. You'll select a partner or spouse for reasons other than a true inner affinity. You'll pay too much attention to what others think and not nearly enough to what you think. And if you're lucky, before it's too late, you'll be miserable enough to start searching in earnest for who you really are.

"To know" in the Bible means to become one with, as when Adam knew Eve. May you be blessed to learn who you are and then become that person as fully as you can.

> **Good-Living Principle 39:**
> **WISE UP by getting to know who you are.**

Optional Exercises

1. Who are you really? Journal on this fundamental question for 15 minutes, then go have a cup of coffee and share your discoveries with a close friend.

2. Interview someone who seems really together. Journal on what you learned from them about becoming and being the person one really is.

3. Write yourself a letter on how to become more fully you.

40 LoveYourself

> People who
> don't love
> themselves
> threaten the
> neighborhood.
> *original proverb*

Jesus' great command to love our neighbors as ourselves is dangerous. After all, what happens if we hate ourselves? Jesus told us about that too. We tend to see our own faults in others rather than ourselves. Psychologists later called this behavior projection.

So, if we don't love ourselves, our neighbors—all people who come into contact with us—are in trouble. The less we love ourselves, the deeper the trouble. Neighbors beware!

The problem is, you can't love yourself if you're unlovable. That's how we are made. What to do?

The answer is simple, even though following through is hard. You have to become lovable. This process takes work. In addition, we are usually our own toughest critics. We can't sweep ourselves off our feet. Flowers and nights on the town do absolutely nothing for us. It's a matter of working on ourselves continuously so that, little by little, we begin to respect ourselves.

We can start doing things for others that they like. We can become considerate of their values and feelings. We can be active listeners for anyone talking with us. We can keep all our promises—a practice usually requiring that we under-promise so that we can over-deliver. Whatever it takes, we need to do it. The alternatives are scary.

Good-Living Principle 40:
WISE UP by learning to love yourself.

Optional Exercises

1. How lovable are you? Discuss this question as objectively as you can in your journal.

2. What things might you do to become more lovable? Advise yourself in a letter.

3. Write an essay describing the most lovable person you know. What is it about him or her that causes others to love them?

Follow Your Dream

> Where there is no vision, the people perish.
> *Proverbs 29:18*

This goes for individuals too. To live day to day without a vision is merely to exist.

Bloody Mary in *South Pacific* puts the matter positively: "You got to have a dream, / If you no have a dream, / How you gonna have a dream come true?"

Everything begins with your call. You feel moved to go somewhere or do something, like the Biblical Abraham, who was impelled to leave his homeland for an unknown country and found a new people.

The need for a vision is so important that Native Americans require young people to undergo a vision quest. With assistance from elders, youth prepare themselves physically and spiritually to spend time alone in the wilderness. Usually, they go for several days and nights with only a blanket and the clothes on their backs. No compass, no water, no food. They seek out a "power place." If fortunate, they will have a dream or dramatic experience that guides them the rest of their lives.

But having a dream isn't enough. You also have to follow it. "If you want your dreams to come true," says a Yiddish proverb, "don't sleep." Will Rogers, the late-19th-Century American humorist, put it this way: "Even if you're on the right track, you'll get run over if you just sit there."

So, begin by seeking your vision. Then, carry it out.

> **Good-Living Principle 41:**
> **WISE UP by following your dream.**

Optional Exercises

1. Do you have a vision? Spend fifteen minutes writing about it in your journal.

2. Share with a friend on how far you've come toward realizing your life-goal(s).

3. Write yourself a letter on next steps for achieving your dream.

Be Practical

42

> Think of many things—do one.
>
> *Portuguese proverb*

Some people have great ideas. They just never do them. There are lots of blueprints, but construction never results.

Now having good ideas is a wonderful place to start. But having too many may be worse than having too few. The inspirations trample each other getting out the door.

So, step one: Sort your ideas out and write each one up in a few sentences. Be as clear as you can. Step two: Let your descriptions sit for a few days. Step three: Read what you have written and circle your favorite proposal. Step four: Leave the ideas alone for another few days. Step five: Re-read your ideas and put a star by the one you like best. Step six: Write yourself a letter in which you try to talk yourself out of this choice. Step seven: Discuss your top idea with friends and get their constructive feedback. Step eight: Make an action plan in which you break the idea down into a series of activities. Step nine: If the idea will cost money, consult with business friends unafraid to say what they think. Step ten: If you still like your idea, go for it.

Better one thing well done than fifty great ideas. The way to failure is paved with unrealized projects. Success requires focus, planning, and hard work. So, choose carefully, get your feet on the ground, and walk.

> **Good-Living Principle 42:**
> **WISE UP by being practical.**

Optional Exercises

1. How are you at following through on project ideas? Discuss this question in your journal.

2. Who is the most practical person you know? Draft an essay about him or her.

3. Write yourself a letter with suggestions on how to become more practical.

43 Do Your Own Thing

> Live your own
> life, for you
> will die your
> own death.
> *Latin proverb*

This is easy advice for most
"First World" people these days.
Individualism seems instinctual with
us. The 60's only made it stronger.

Still, we Americans live with many
forces that would like us to conform.
Often our elders have strong ideas
about what we should or shouldn't
do. Modern Western parents, though
permissive, still try to influence their
kids' choices of friends, relationships,
lifestyles, and careers.

Then there's peer pressure. If you
look at how people dress or the
music they prefer, it's clear that
what's in still determines what's on.
Individualism may be valued, but
fashion rules.

True individualism is knowing your
potential, then working to become
the person you really are. If something comes easy and brings you joy,
those are good indications of your
gifts. Don't put them aside because

many others in your family, say, were lawyers. If that idea turns you off while you feel great drawing or painting, look for a career in the arts.

Scott Peck, the psychiatrist, writes about how miserable he was at the family prep school in New England. When he quit in favor of a Quaker day school in New York City, where he lived, he began enjoying school and life. What about you? Do you follow the beat of others, or do you march to your own drummer?

> **Good-Living Principle 43:**
> **WISE UP by doing your own thing.**

Optional Exercises

1. Are you doing your own thing or someone else's? Discuss this question in your journal.

2. Get together with a friend and talk about the strongest individuals you know.

3. Journal on one decision you could make now to help you become the real you.

Be a Team Player

> One star
> can't make a
> constellation.
> *original saying*

Lots of American kids want to be "stars." Ah, to be Michael Jordan or the President of the United States! Maybe kids everywhere think like this.

Confucian cultures, by contrast, emphasize being part of the group. "The nail that sticks out gets hammered in," the Japanese say. Not only that but when you introduce yourself on behalf of your company, you'll state something like "Honda's Matsumoto wishes to talk with Saito-san." For all intents and purposes, you belong to the company, from dress code to values. Come to think of it, your last name as a Japanese comes before your first—emphasizing that family comes first too.

In the West we do well with sports where individuals compete—diving, skiing, track and field. When it comes to team sports, from basketball to football to doubles in tennis, our coaches always emphasize teamwork. The Michael Jordans of the world can't win games all by themselves. How effective when the star unexpectedly passes to a less prestigious player who happens to be open! Scores usually result.

The reality is that Japan can't get along without stars any more than America can without teamwork. It takes balance between the two for groups of people to achieve goals, whether winning a sports contest or building a car.

Still, we Western individualists need to remember the power of the group.

> **Good-Living Principle 44:**
> **WISE UP by being a team player.**

Optional Exercises

1. Are you a team player or a rugged individualist? Discuss this question in your journal.

2. Write an essay or journal entry on your most effective group experience.

3. Write yourself a letter with advice on how to become a better team player.

Trust What You See

Saint Thomas, the great doubter in Christian tradition, refused to accept his friends' story that Jesus had returned from the dead. Until he saw it with his own eyes, he'd keep his options open. Then Jesus appeared. Thomas still wasn't sure what was what. Jesus invited Thomas to feel his (Jesus') wounds, which Thomas did. Then (and only then) did Thomas believe.

Doubting Thomas is the patron saint of science, where seeing—by lots of people, not just one—is believing. He is also the unofficial patron of the U.S. State of Missouri, the "Show Me" State. "I'm from Missouri," goes the tagline. "I've got to be shown."

The other way people put this idea is "I'll believe it when I see it." In other words, personal experience is for many the highest standard of proof.

Not surprisingly, the English words *evidence* and *evident* come from the Latin verb *videre*, "to see."

Columbus apparently believed the world was round before he set forth on his first voyage. His men weren't so sure and probably panicked a bit as they approached their first horizon. But when they kept approaching new horizons and none of their three ships fell over the edge, they had to accept that the world wasn't flat after all. They were blind, so to speak, but now they saw.

> **Good-Living Principle 45:**
> **WISE UP by believing what you see.**

Optional Exercises

1. Do you tend to take things on faith, or do you prefer to see things first for yourself? Journal on this question.

2. Write about something you witnessed which was hard to believe. Why?

3. Imagine what it would be like to be blind; then have a conversation with a friend.

Don't Believe Appearances

> Everything is about something else.
> *Varindra Vittachi,*
> *d. 1993*

The world is flat. It must be. After all, look at it from the highest mountain you can scale. Seeing, as they say, is believing.

Who in their right mind would have accompanied Columbus on his first voyage? Imagine sailing out to the edge of the world; then getting killed by falling off.

So much for the vision test! It's as if we walk around with defective eyesight; then claim whatever we see as truth. Or are colorblind persons who insist that red is green. Seeing may be believing, but can we always believe what we see?

Maybe this is the reason many of us prefer day to night. In daytime you can see clearly, whereas at night, unless you have artificial light, you can't. But night may be getting a bum rap. Think about it. Night is the time of quiet, reflection, and rest. Daytime is when we rush about, getting and spending, fighting with our boss, and (if we are not careful) getting skin cancer.

Not everything we think good is good. Not everything we think bad is bad. Up is usually considered positive, while we tend to take down as a negative. But if cats or children climb too high and suddenly find themselves literally up a tree, being "down and out" starts looking pretty good. So don't judge by appearances. The reality could be different.

> **Good-Living Principle 46:**
> **WISE UP by not taking things at face value.**

Optional Exercises

1. Write about a time when something you thought true turned out not to be.

2. Has a friend ever changed your mind? Journal about it.

3. Put on someone else's glasses. Then discuss the experience with another person.

Get It off Your Chest

47

When the heart is at ease, the body is healthy.
Chinese saying

The best way to live is to keep your heart unburdened. If you walk around with a heavy heart, you're generally carrying more than you should.

The Catholic Church includes the rites of Confession and Absolution. These practices give individuals the chance to get rid of their inner burdens and start over. Better to fess up than to break down. Troubles kept inside can build until an individual explodes in anger and frustration or, more commonly, becomes depressed or physically ill.

Sharing in Twelve Step and other support groups serves the same purpose. Somehow, airing your troubles publicly to a group of attentive, non-judgmental peers works magic. People who come to a meeting angry or crying often leave smiling or laughing.

In Islam, after fasting during the month of Ramadan, it's the practice in some traditions for individuals to ask each other's forgiveness for anything they might have done during the past year, consciously or unconsciously, that harmed or upset the other person. While this custom can become mechanical, inner healing often takes place on both sides. The requirement in Twelve Step programs to make amends to those we have harmed has the same purpose and effect.

The point is, don't stuff disappointment, hurt, or guilt but purge them.

> **Good-Living Principle 47:**
> **WISE UP by getting it off your chest.**

Optional Exercises

1. How do you deal with troubles? Are you the strong, silent type, or do you look for consolation and advice from others? Answer these questions in your journal.

2. Write an essay about the techniques you use to keep your heart light.

3. Interview someone who seems upbeat most of the time. Write about how they do it.

48 Don't Whine

> Instead of complaining about what's wrong, be grateful for what's right.
>
> *Source unknown*

Crying is one thing. Whining is another. Getting things off your chest is not the same as bellyaching.

By lightening your emotional load, crying helps you get on with living. Whining, however, keeps you from facing your troubles and moving on. It is an unproductive substitute for action. And not a very pleasant one for those nearby.

Chronic complainers have few friends. First, they never take responsibility for anything. Others or the system or the government or the Communists or the Capitalists or fate or God or the Devil are to blame. Never they themselves. They try to excuse themselves by pointing the finger elsewhere.

Whining is a habit many of us pick up in childhood. After all, infants get the help they need by crying. Later, when we're bigger, sometimes with a new baby in the house, we whine to keep the spotlight on us. Sooner or later, most of us grow up. We know that whining is for babies, and we don't do it anymore. Still, the temptation lingers.

So, cry when you have to. It's a normal and natural thing to do. But whining is a form of manipulation unacceptable in mature adults. Be grateful for what you have. Work to change what you don't like. But never ever whine.

> **Good-Living Principle 48:**
> **WISE UP by not whining.**

Optional Exercises

1. Audit your behavior for a week. Make a mental note every time you complain. At the end of the week, comment on what sparks your complaining.

2. Go on a "complaint diet" for a day. Journal about the experience before bed.

3. Interview a friend who rarely complains. Ask how they do it and copy them.

Go with the Flow

> Let go and
> let God.
> *Twelve Step slogan*

"If your camel breaks down," the Arabs say, "use your donkey." A Latin proverb offers similar advice: "If the wind dies, take to your oars." In other words, if you want to drive yourself crazy, insist on things going your way all the time. They won't.

Our human will is a wonderful tool. Nothing would get done without it. But not everything we want to do will prove doable, or at least not the way we want it done or within our timeframe. Something has to give. Generally that thing will be us.

Reinhold Niebuhr's Serenity Prayer is based on this hard reality. It goes, "God, grant me the serenity to accept the things I cannot change, courage to change the things I can, and wisdom to know the difference."

Native Americans talk about swimming to the middle of a river to get the best lift from the current. First find the flow. Then allow it to take you in the direction of the stream.

If you must swim against the current, take this advice from Hawaii's lifeguards. A riptide is often too strong for even the best swimmer to move against. Fortunately, riptides are only about 30 feet across. So, swim laterally for about ten meters. Then try to swim in. If you've gotten beyond the tide's width, you should have no problem.

Good-Living Principle 49:
WISE UP by going with the flow.

Optional Exercises

1. Do things always have to go your way, or can you go with the flow? Respond in your journal.

2. Have you discovered techniques "to let go and let God"? Write about them.

3. Can people learn to relax? Argue the case pro or con in an essay.

50 Be Peace

> Carpenters can't build tables better than themselves.
> *Javanese proverb*

Thich Nath Hanh, a Vietnamese Buddhist monk now in his seventies, has a book with this title: *Be Peace*. In other words, it's not possible for warlike people to go out and make peace. What you end up creating will last about as long as a ceasefire between the Israelis and the Palestinians.

In other words, if you want peace on earth, you'd better start with yourself. The song has it right: "Let there be peace on earth, / And let it begin with me." Other options won't work.

Of course, even if you accept this premise, you're stuck with a puzzle: How do you become a peaceful person in the first place? Is anger management enough, or is something more needed?

Military organizations the world over have tried-and-true techniques for turning the boy-next-door into an efficient killing machine. But what institutions can take ordinary short-fused humans and make them into gentle, tolerant beings?

A saying of the Buddha suggests an answer: "If each of us became truly aware of our mortality, we would settle all our differences peacefully." Today the Martin Luther King and Carter Centers in Atlanta, the Mediation Project at Harvard Law School, Peace University in Costa Rica, and the Center for Global Nonviolence in Honolulu all offer training. Maybe each school, church, temple, and mosque should do so too.

> **Good-Living Principle 50:**
> **WISE UP by being the peace you want for the world.**

Optional Exercises

1. How peaceable are you? Reflect on how often and vehemently you argue; then assess your "peace quotient" in your journal.

2. Read William Ury's *The Third Side* and write a book report for class.

3. Search the Internet for "peace academies" and share your findings at school.

51 Keep Learning

> I grow old learning something new every day.
>
> *Solon, c. 630 – c. 560 B.C.E.*

According to Richard Bolles in *The Three Boxes of Life*, Americans divide life into three parts: youth for learning, the middle years for earning, and old age for leisure. Education is preparation. After graduation we get on with living. We make money, find spouses, have children, buy houses, develop portfolios, and retire. After that, we visit castles in France, drink wine on the Rhine, and sunbathe in Waikiki. After that, well, we don't talk about after that.

Bolles suggests that we should instead think of learning throughout life, doing meaningful work—whether paid or volunteered—until we can't, and mixing in leisure from cradle to grave. Not three side-by-side boxes, he argues, but three strands woven neatly together is what life should be be about.

Of course, we don't stop learning when we get our high school, college, or professional-school diplomas. On-the-job training is the name of the game everywhere. Some professions even require continuing education to maintain a license.

The real point, though, is we need to keep learning about life itself and the art of living. Gold doesn't lie around on the streets. We have to search for it. Wisdom doesn't come free. We have to earn it. So, keep living, keep loving, and keep learning. The riches we find will be ourselves.

Good-Living Principle 51:
WISE UP by becoming a lifelong learner.

Optional Exercises

1. Write an essay about your concepts of school and teacher. Where does school take place and who are our real teachers?

2. Interview the best lifelong learner you know. Share that person's approach with a friend.

3. Journal on three things you plan to do in the near-future to become a wiser person.

52 Choose

> Choosing
> is a form
> of suffering.
> *[Wer die Wahl
> hal, hat die Qual.]*
> German saying

Wisdom comes from two Anglo-Saxon roots. The *Wis-* part is related to the modern German *Wissen*, "to know." *Dom* comes from the Old English *deman*, "to judge." In modern English we have the word *deem* ("believe or judge, especially after deliberation"). Thus wisdom means something like making good choices based on [sufficient] knowledge.

According to some etymologists, *wis* itself derives from the Latin *visio*, the act of seeing, or vision. That's why, according to Ralph Waldo Emerson, a "seer" is both someone who sees *and* a sage—a person with *insight*.

Many readings in this book seem to contradict each other. "Go for It!" vs. "Wait a Minute!," "Attend to the Details" vs. "Get the Big Picture," "Celebrate Commonalities" vs. "Celebrate Difference," etc. How can you negotiate these apparent contradictions?

Nils Bohr, the 20th-Century physicist, once said, "The opposite of truth is a lie. But the opposite of one great truth is another great truth." In the game of life, timing is everything. Remember Ecclesiastes' advice in the Bible: There's a time to be born and a time to die, a time to plant and a time to harvest. In the end, it's all about when and how we apply the great principles of living.

So, choose well. The life you save will be your own.

> **Good-Living Principle 52:**
> **WISE UP by making good choices.**

Optional Exercises

1. How do you make major choices? Do you do your "due diligence" or prefer to make "executive decisions"? Discuss this question in your journal.

2. Write about the wisest choice you've made. Why do you think it was wise?

3. Discuss strategies for making life choices with a classmate or friend.

53 Work

If you don't do it, it won't get done. There's a clear relationship between input and output. So, you'd better do something if you want something done.

Most religious people, regardless of their faith, believe in prayer. They ask for this or that hoped-for outcome from a spiritual power. Sometimes they use a traditional formula. Sometimes they ask free-form. Yet Saint Benedict, the Sixth-Century founder of the Benedictine Catholic Order, reportedly said, "To work is to pray."

In other words, asking is good. But it will take you only so far. After that, you need to roll up your sleeves and start sweating.

Work, according to the Jewish and Christian Scriptures, came as God's punishment for Adam and Eve's disobedience in Eden. In the beginning, our First Parents got caught eating the forbidden apple. The result: A life sentence of hard labor.

Of course, labor doesn't have to be hard. A good attitude helps. You can love work that corresponds to your talents and is fulfilling. Or you can like the results—a neat room, for instance, where it is more pleasant to live. Or you can see all work as a way to build character or practice discipline. Pumping iron doesn't only cause you to sweat; it builds your body and helps you look better on the beach.

So, bottomline: Work is a necessity. But if you view it right, it is also a blessing.

> **Good-Living Principle 53:**
> **WISE UP by working.**

Optional Exercises

1. Write about your work ethic in a class essay or your journal.

2. Describe your work role model to a classmate or friend.

3. What work do you hate? Journal about how you might get over this dislike?

54 Play

> All work and
> no play makes
> Jack a dull boy.
> *English saying*

This proverb probably rhymed once. It doesn't anymore. In puritanical Anglo-American society we've lost our ability to play.

Play is for kids. Come to think of it, shouldn't they be learning to read by five and thinking about good colleges by ten?

To be idle is to invite the Devil. So we create make-work. We do anything. We just don't play.

What is play anyway? We could respond with Louis Armstrong. When someone asked him what jazz was, he replied, "Man, if you gotta ask you'll never know."

Webster's Desk Dictionary of the English Language (1990) includes this definition: "Fun or jest, as opposed to seriousness." That's it. Be serious, or go play!

Come to think of it, play is like jazz. It's improv. It's doing what we feel like doing when we feel like doing it, as the spirit moves us. It's doing our thing our way. It's our inner self running through the fields or dancing free. It's play, and sadly we don't do enough of it for our own good. Or else we come at it like a project, plan it to death, and lose all its benefits.

So remember to include lots of play in your life. You can even be playful in the midst of something serious. Just don't work too hard at it.

Good-Living Principle 54:
WISE UP by playing regularly.

Optional Exercises

1. How are you at playing? Journal about it. Or, come to think of it, forget it. Just go play somewhere!

2. Now, sit down and comment on how you feel after having had some good fun.

3. Write about the most playful adult you know? What are the lessons for you?

55 Forgive

> If anyone wrongs you, exercise forgiveness and patiently dismiss the matter. For if you take the wrong to heart, you hurt no one but yourself.
>
> *Mennonite advice*

This wisdom is at the heart of Christianity. Yet it goes against some inner grain and is very hard to practice.

Much closer to home is our instinct for revenge. When something bad is done to us, we want to get our own back with interest.

We all resemble Israelis and Palestinians in this regard. Forgiveness? Forget it! How about a counter-raid that takes even more lives? We'll show them what it costs to do something bad to us!

So much for turning the other cheek. Yet sooner or later the feuding must stop. How much better a United States of Europe than a Hundred Year War! Germany and France, those perennial foes, are great friends now. What a shame these ethnically related neighbors had to kill and maim millions of each other's citizens—men, women, and children—to get to the point of "normal relations"!

In Twelve Step Programs members conclude that one of the people they have offended and harmed the most is themselves. If they want to make amends, that is often the best place to start. The same is probably true for nations.

Forgiving another is never easy, but the fruits are sweet. Holding a grudge, on the other hand, hurts mainly ourselves and often innocent bystanders as well.

> **Good-Living Principle 55:**
> **WISE UP by forgiving.**

Optional Exercises

1. How are you at forgiving others? Yourself? Comment in your journal.

2. Is there someone out there you need to forgive? Make a plan and go for it!

3. Write about a vengeful acquaintance. Why don't you want to be like him or her?

56

Just Say "I'm Sorry"

It takes a lot to apologize. It took King Lear, an old man, five acts of exile and betrayal to beg forgiveness from his loyal daughter, Cordelia.

It's hard to say "I'm sorry" at any age. Sometimes, of course, we may even be right. But our obstinacy in maintaining our position ends up alienating the other person. So, right or not, we have still committed a wrong.

What good does it do us to win an argument at the cost of someone else's feelings?

The Twelve Step Programs make a point of advising members to apologize. According to Step 10, "[we] continued to take personal inventory and when we were wrong promptly admitted it."

Some marriage guidebooks counsel newlyweds never to go to bed with an argument unsettled. Whatever the rights or wrongs in the case, the relationship comes first. That's why it's important for the young spouses to apologize as quickly as possible.

In Eric Segal's *Love Story*, one of the main characters comments, "When you are in love, you never have to say you're sorry," or words to that effect. If people take that maxim to heart, the divorce rate will never drop.

> **Good-Living Principle 56:**
> **WISE UP by apologizing promptly for your wrongs.**

Optional Exercises

1. How are you at apologizing soon after you have done something wrong? Write on this topic in your journal.

2. Share views with a friend on what makes it hard to say, "I'm sorry."

3. Are there times when you shouldn't apologize? Respond to this question in a brief essay.

57 Give and Take

> Hands that give also receive.
> *Ecuadorian Proverb*

This is another of those golden-mean lessons. Don't give all the time. That leads to burnout or becoming a doormat. But don't take all the time either.

A friend of ours, a Portuguese architect, likes to show the gesture of an open hand moving back and forward between himself and another person. "You see," he comments, "the gesture to give and the gesture to receive are really the same."

Consider conversing. You talk, you listen, you talk, you listen. Mouth and ears alternate. The sender becomes the receiver and vice versa. Good conversation is a matter of give-and-take. So is good living.

Equal relationships are built on this principle of oscillation. So is egalitarian government, where officials both lead and serve the people they represent. It's not a matter of masters and slaves—all take for one and all give for the other. No, we're talking about win/win relationships, where both sides lead and follow by turns.

For example, legislators develop the language for a referendum on a proposed constitutional amendment. Then, at the next general election, the public determines whether or not to ratify it. The lawmakers must follow the will of the electorate.

Life is full of dynamic opposites—waking and sleeping, working and resting, learning and applying, etc. It's an alternating current, so learn to go with the flow.

**Good-Living Principle 57:
WISE UP by giving and taking.**

Optional Exercises

1. Assess your relationships in terms of give-and-take. Are there some in which this dynamic is out of balance? Journal on this question.

2. Suggest in a paper how to improve this dynamic in the classroom or work place.

3. Discuss with a friend your experience of give-and-take between the sexes.

58 Just Say Yes

The Power of Positive Thinking wasn't a huge bestseller for nothing. This grandparent of self-improvement books helped Americans turn their country into today's lone super power.

"If you can conceive it and believe it you can achieve it," wrote Napoleon Hill. A few decades later, Jesse Jackson, the African American leader, encouraged his followers with this refrain.

Hill, at the request of the elderly Andrew Carnegie, made a study of America's most successful self-made "men." (And they were all men too.) What was the key to their achievements? He later shared what he learned in a book called *Think and Grow Rich*. The secret, he said, was "positive mental attitude."

Shortened to PMA, this concept became the basis of a training program fostered by the late billionaire E. Clement Stone. Be positive—think positively—and you will move mountains. Conceive . . . believe . . . achieve.

While an affirmative attitude may not solve all problems, it will take you a lot farther than a carping "Yes, but" approach to life. And it will certainly beat the "No way, José!" stance hands down. Prophecies we repeat inside our heads have a way of fulfilling themselves.

So be positive. Say yes to life no matter what. You'll still need to do your part. But the results should make you happy.

Good-Living Principle 58:
WISE UP by being positive.

Optional Exercises

1. Do you say yes to life, or are you a Yes-But or No-Way-José type of person? Analyze yourself along these lines in your journal.

2. Write about three (3) things you might do to have a more positive attitude.

3. Interview the most affirming person you know. Write about what you learn.

59 Just Say No

Being accommodating is fine, but sometimes you need to say no and mean it. Knowing when is essential.

Here are some clues from the world's treasury of wisdom. First, if something seems too good to be true, it probably is. Go with your gut, not your heart. Be prudent. Just say no.

If it's something your grandmother wouldn't have done at your age, think twice before going forward. Who is likely to benefit or suffer? If the cost to anyone is too high, just say no. If the deal's not win/win, it's not worth making.

If something is illegal, no matter what the potential benefits, don't pursue it. If the law doesn't get you, your conscience will—or should.

Perhaps the most important place to say no is when someone is trying to get you to do something that doesn't fit you. No matter how much a job pays, if you have no heart or talent for it, don't take it. You'll be unhappy in a month, miserable in six, if you do. Figure out who you are and what you're good at. Then find or create a job that fits. When it comes to anything else, just say no. The same is true of relationships.

Learn what's good for you, and when the opportunity arises, say yes with gusto. To everything else, just say no.

Good-Living Principle 59:
WISE UP by learning to say no.

Optional Exercises

1. Do you seek approval by saying yes more than you should? Respond in the privacy of your journal.

2. Write yourself a letter advising how to decide when to accept or reject an offer.

3. Are there people who say no too much? Write about one without using his/her name.

Wising UP 145

Take Your Turn

> To everything there is a season. . . .
>
> *Ecclesiastes 3:1*

Queue up. Get in line. Your turn will come in due course.

Nothing is worse than a mob scene. People crowding in to get theirs. People trampling each other to get out of a burning theater.

The last case is understandable. It's natural to panic in a life-threatening situation. Yet the reality is, we'd all have a better chance to get out safely if we'd stayed calm and taken our turn.

Taking one's turn is not only a matter of fairness or, in extreme situations, safety. It's also a matter of our time versus "God's time." Our time is based on the all-too-human desire to get what we want now. It's instant gratification. My way or the highway.

God's time is based on ripeness. When the fruit is ripe, it will fall from the branch by itself. Things ripen at their own pace. I can pull green apples off the tree, but I can't force them to become sweet before their time.

So, taking our turn depends on being patient—allowing all things the freedom to ripen according to their own laws and schedules.

The writer of Ecclesiastes was right to remind us that "there is a time to every purpose under heaven." Every dog will have its day.

> **Good-Living Principle 60:**
> **WISE UP by taking your turn.**

Optional Exercises

1. How are you at awaiting your turn? Are you willing to be patient, or do you try to crash the line? Discuss these questions in your journal.

2. Write on what you've learned about "due seasons" from life experiences to date.

3. Discuss with a friend or colleague why taking your turn is ultimately a matter of justice.

61 Take a Walk

The British talk about taking "constitutionals." A nice walk regularly taken can really set you up. It helps digestion too. Hence the after-dinner stroll.

The Latin culture, which can be credited with the siesta, also gave us walks. The Greek way of dealing with problems was to allow time to pass before deciding. In night, they said, was counsel. Dreams might offer the right solution. Americans say, "Sleep on it."

Rome, on the other hand, thought an excellent way to deal with conundrums, a Latin word after all, was to ambulate—in plain language, to take a walk. The literal meaning of the proverb, above, is, "You have to walk in order to work out a problem."

Nowadays, of course, books on walking or running as aerobic exercise explain how sustaining a higher heart rate gets the endorphins flowing.

Pretty soon, the problem du jour stops oppressing us and is magically distanced from our consciousness. Sometimes the right answer just seems to pop up. Or else, we somehow stop worrying and can think our way to a viable solution.

Naturally, you don't have to have a problem to take a walk. It's healthful just to get away from our desk, go outside, and move around. The French do their promenades, Germanic peoples take walks in the woods, while Italians and Central Europeans go out at night for a corso. Main thing: Go favor your legs.

Good-Living Principle 61:
WISE UP by taking regular walks.

Optional Exercises

1. Are you a walker? Write about your walking habits in your journal.

2. In a paper, comment on the effect walking has on your life.

3. Go for regular walks with someone and discuss whatever you want.

62 Take a Nap

One short sleep past, we wake eternally....
John Donne, 1573-1631

The *siesta* is one of humankind's greatest inventions. Whoops! Humankind didn't invent it at all. We copied it from our relatives, the (other) animals.

Bears hibernate. But the really great siesta-takers are cats. They take catnaps night and day and are among the most graceful, relaxed, yet attentive creatures on the planet.

Spaniards get credit for the invention, possibly because the word comes from their language. In equatorial countries like India and Indonesia, where it is cooler and more pleasant to be active at night, the afternoon nap is also de rigueur. As Noel Coward instructs us, only mad dogs and Englishmen go out in the mid-day sun.

We eat several times a day. So where did this idea come from that we should sleep only once every 24 hours?

Naps sharpen us for the rest of the day and make us more attentive in the evening. Scientific research in Germany has found that workers who get a half-hour's on-the-job rest each day are more productive. As a result, a growing number of German companies are installing "rest rooms" in the true sense of the word and are permitting employees to bring cots, pillows, and sleeping bags to work. Apparently "sleeping on the job" is not the offense against employers it once was.

Good-Living Principle 62:
WISE UP by taking a nap.

Optional Exercises

1. Do you take naps? How often and for how long? Journal about the effect of this habit on your work.

2. Have you ever lived in a place where siestas are normal? Write a paper about it.

3. If you don't take naps, try it for a week and discuss the impact with a friend.

Hope for the Best

> If it were not for hope, the heart would break. *Greek saying*

"New day—new fate." The Bulgarians say. Each morning an unwritten page is added to your book of life—a new opportunity to create your world. Where there's life, there's hope, or should be.

Hope for the best, but strive toward it too. God is a good worker, according to the Hebrew proverb, but likes to be helped. The Japanese, whose post-War recovery gives them credibility, put it this way: The day you decide to do it is your lucky day.

So do your part and leave the rest to the Universe. Hope keeps you open to the possibilities.

God often visits us, the French say, but usually we are not at home. Hope is about being at home and opening the door. Availability may be two-thirds of success—being in the right place at the right time so good things can happen.

Pessimism, however, may have the opposite effect. It is like turning our earth-receiving dish away from a satellite's signal. Does that mean there's no satellite, no signal? Of course not. But from the perspective of the person not receiving, there may as well not be.

Being hopeful allows our earth-receiving dish to scan the heavens until we pick up a signal. What if there is no signal? You may ask. Unless you scan the heavens, you'll never know. So, take a chance. Be optimistic. Try.

> **Good-Living Principle 63:**
> **WISE UP by being hopeful.**

Optional Exercises

1. Are you an optimist or a pessimist? Respond in your journal.

2. Interview an optimistic friend. Write an essay on how optimism impacts their life.

3. Try being more optimistic for a week; then discuss the results with a friend.

64 Prepare for the Worst

> Trust in Allah but tie your camel. *Arabic saying*

The equivalent in English is more war-like: Trust in God but keep your powder dry. Wet gun powder won't ignite. Hence you'll be unable to defend yourself against your enemies. The Arabs, living in deserts, knew they would be lost without their camels. The animals might stay at an oasis without being tethered. But why chance it? The alternative could be deadly.

We roll up our windows and lock our cars when we park. Some of us even add a protective bar so that our steering wheels can't be used. Still others will pay extra for cars equipped with a burglar alarm or will have one installed soon after purchase.

You can never be too careful. Hope for the best but prepare for the worst.

Going to Indonesia? Morocco? France? Are your shots up to date? Better check. Better invest the $100 and have a sore arm for a week. You just never know.

Plan to retire one day? Think your government pension is sufficient? Think again. Who knows if those funds will even be there when you retire? Better diversify. Stock owners beware. Markets are unpredictable. Employees with lots of company shares should take special care. Think of Enron and stuff your mattress with gold coins. Remember the Boy Scout motto: Be prepared!

> **Good-Living Principle 64:**
> **WISE UP by preparing for the worst.**

Optional Exercises

1. Do you tend to put all your eggs into one basket? How might you plan better for an uncertain future? Use your journal to strategize.

2. Chat with a friend about how you check your house before leaving on a trip.

3. Write yourself a letter on areas where you need to prepare better for the worst.

65 Do It Anyway

Some things you just have to do, like it or not. Eating and sleeping come to mind, but they are generally rather pleasant.

Other things, though, are really not much fun. Studying for final exams, then taking them is an example. Or searching for a job in a bad labor market.

Living in a family, in society, means having to share time, space, and energy with others. No wonder some people choose not to get married, have a pet, or have kids. Yet in this regard, simply to be alive is to be compromised. Think about work.

The obvious answer is, if you can't get out of something, get into it. See how you can make the situation work for you. You have to study for exams, right? Get a good study group together so you can decide collectively on the most important topics; then ask each

other questions. Got to do the dishes?
Make it a game to see how skillfully
you can load the dishwasher, or, better
yet, do it with someone else so you can
while away the time with conversation.
It's surprising how quickly and pleasant-
ly chores can be handled when you turn
them into fun.

Someone who's learned the art of living
can brighten up even the drabbest task.

Good-Living Principle 65:
WISE UP by doing unpleasant
but necessary things with style.

Optional Exercises

1. How are you when it comes to
   handling life's unpleasant chores?
   Write in response to this question in
   your journal.

2. Who in your circle does this sort
   of thing best? Interview them for their
   secret.

3. Try "getting into" unpleasant tasks
   for a week; then write about the experience.

Don't Argue About Taste

A German woman we know has lived in Hawaii for years. When she visits her homeland, she is criticized for dressing too brightly. Such colors, she is told, are not seemly for a woman her age.

Taste is often a national matter. East Indians combine colors in ways unthinkable in the West. Indonesian men and women both wear sarongs, wrap-around garments for the lower body that Occidentals would consider for women only. And Scotsmen, when donning national dress, wear skirts, called kilts.

The ancient Romans long ago learned that it is fruitless to argue about taste. One person's meat is another's poison. The penicillin that heals here can kill there—if the person is allergic.

Concepts of beauty also differ. You wonder how this person could have fallen in love with that person, or why so-and-so fixed up their house to look so "dark and cluttered." Beauty, clearly, is in the eye of the beholder.

So, don't waste your time arguing with a friend that so-and-so is not good for them or a particular dress makes them look fat. You might end up losing a friend. If they want your opinion, they'll ask. And even then, be diplomatic. If the person makes a mistake, it's their mistake and they are entitled to it.

Remember: There's no disputing taste.

Good-Living Principle 66:
WISE UP by letting others follow their own taste.

Optional Exercises

1. How do you like it when others try to influence your selection of clothing, furniture, friends? Comment in your journal.

2. Have you ever imperiled a relationship by being judgmental? Write about it.

3. If you have to criticize another's choice, share some ways to do it diplomatically.

Don't Boss Others Around

> A gentle hand may lead even an elephant by a hair.
>
> *Iranian proverb*

What a tough lesson! Especially for parents and other "leaders."

Adults are responsible, right? If their children are wild in public, people will consider them poor parents. Or, if someone's staff fails to reach their goals, the executive will call their manager, not them, onto the carpet. "Why can't you get your staff to do their job?" The CEO will ask.

Yet the best supervisors don't boss people around. They delegate, provide explicit directions and expectations tions, coach where necessary, check in periodically, and hold their employ accountable. They make it clear that if a project fails, the entire company will suffer. But if it succeeds, everyone will share in the success.

Good parenting works the same way. Children need examples, not lectures. If you want them to be good listeners, model that behavior. If you want them to be respectful, show them respect. If you want them to speak gently to others, speak gently to them.

An ounce of suggestion is worth a pound of command. Robert Redford in the film *The Horse Whisperer* could tame the most obstreperous animals by putting his face next to theirs and talking gently. Praising activities you like and thanking people for something they've done will reinforce that behavior more effectively than blaming or shaming.

Good-Living Principle 67:
WISE UP by helping others to do their best.

Optional Exercises

1. How are you at managing people? Are you overly controlling, or do you delegate and work with others to achieve their goals? Comment in your journal.

2. Write a comparative essay on your best and worse supervisor.

3. Send yourself a letter on how to become a better leader.

68 Choose Friends Wisely

There are lots of things in life we *can't* choose: our parents, gender, country of origin, even our astrological sign. But we can choose our friends.

Of course, there's no guarantee we'll choose individuals who'll help bring out the best in us. The world's proverbs offer caution. Birds of a feather flock together. In other words, if you're fairly mature, you're likely to choose mature friends. If you're not, beware.

This is where danger lurks. If you lie down with dogs, the English say, you'll rise up with fleas. And a Bulgarian proverb warns, if you call one wolf, you invite the pack. Even one rotten apple can ruin the whole bushel.

So watch out for the fast crowd. Don't hang around with folks who snort coke or spike their raves with Ecstasy. The life you save may be your own.

Prince Hal, later Henry the Fifth of England, spent his youth with the wrong people—Falstaff and his gang of thieves. Fortunately, Hal figured things out before it was too late and became a national hero. As an adolescent he was the prototype of today's royal teenagers, spoiled kids with enough money and privileges to get into trouble. At least Hal grew up to be Henry.

So, don't shackle yourself to friends who pull you down. You do have a choice.

> **Good-Living Principle 68:**
> **WISE UP by choosing excellent friends.**

Optional Exercises

1. In your journal, inventory the quality of the people you spend the most time with. Are you doing yourself a service?

2. Comment there on how your best friend helps you become your best self.

3. Write a short essay on the characteristics of a truly good friend.

69 Work on Yourself

> Conquering an army is hard, O Monks, but conquering yourself is harder still.
>
> *A saying of the Buddha*

Deferred maintenance refers to postponed care for a building or piece of property. Usually the care is needed. Lack of money generally causes the postponement.

If you don't change the oil periodically, your car will become unusable. When it comes to care for ourselves, deferred maintenance is also a problem. Whether the focus be body, mind, emotions, or soul, neglect can lead to dangerous consequences.

Put positively, we must work on ourselves continually. We have to keep our bodies well-fed, rested, and in shape. But we can't stop there. Our minds need to be regularly stocked and exercised too. As the United Negro College Fund reminds us, "A mind is a terrible thing to waste." Yet even a sharp mind in a healthy body is not enough if our emotions ride roughshod over us and others. Dr. Daniel Goleman has recently taught us about emotional intelligence. We must develop and maintain maturity in this realm as well.

Finally, there is the matter of spiritual well-being. Belonging to a formal religion can be helpful. But membership alone is not sufficient. You have to have an ongoing, growing relationship with Spirit. You and your Higher Power have to be in constant, intimate contact.

In short, don't neglect yourself. Find effective ways to maintain who you are.

**Good-Living Principle 69:
WISE UP by working on yourself.**

Optional Exercises

1. What parts of yourself are you best at maintaining—body, mind, emotions, spirit? Where do you need work? Respond in your journal.

2. Interview someone who seems really together. Ask them how they do it.

3. Draft a realistic plan for self-improvement; then discuss it with a friend.

Live Aloha

> A life without love is like a year without summer.
>
> *Swedish proverb*

Here in Hawaii we are blessed with endless summer. Maybe that's why we get along so well despite our racial diversity. Only a fifth of our 1.2 million residents are white. More than half our marriages cross ethnic lines.

Our nickname is *The Aloha State*. *Aloha*, the Hawaiian word, means sharing *ha*, the breath of life (or spirit), with others. It also means sharing the resources of our small islands— among the most isolated pieces of inhabited real estate on earth—with our fellow residents. In fact, Hawaii lies in the middle of the world's largest ocean. People on islands either get along or leave.

A common local bumper sticker advises us to "Live Aloha." Drivers show respect for other cars by routinely letting them in, an action acknowledged with a friendly wave. We also refrain from using our horns except in emergencies. Once, during a hotel strike, residents answered a call by the local newspapers and opened their homes to "visitors," our name for tourists.

Planet Earth is an island too, floating in the huge sea of space and—thanks to technology and population growth—getting smaller by the day. We have to find ways to live together or else. Sharing Aloha is not a bad place to start.

Good-Living Principle 70:
WISE UP by learning to live Aloha.

Optional Exercises

1. How are you at sharing with and caring for others? Is your Aloha Spirit limited, or does it encompass the whole world? Discuss these questions in your journal.

2. Write a paper on a public figure who seems to exemplify the Aloha Spirit.

3. Brainstorm in a small group how people might show Aloha in their daily lives.

71 Move on

Keep on
keepin' on.
*African-American
saying*

Life is motion. Death is stasis. A famous poem by William Wordsworth talks about his recently deceased beloved: "...No motion has she now, no force, / She neither hears nor sees, / Rolled round in earth's diurnal course, / With rocks, and stones, and trees."

When someone is alive but unable to get on with things, we talk about them as being "stuck," "in a rut," "dead in the water." Sometimes this paralysis is the result of, or reaction to, some traumatic event—a condition now known as "post-traumatic stress disorder," or PTSD.

If you think you are suffering from PTSD, get medical attention. If you are simply in the doldrums, seek the counsel of good friends, talk with a pastoral adviser, start exercising regularly, take an adult-education course on something of interest, begin a regular spiritual practice, help someone else. There are lots of ways out. The initiative, though, has to be yours.

Nothing is sadder than someone tied to the past, unable to turn to the future or embrace and live in the present. Our minds are like the rope that ties a sailboat to the dock. If you want to get somewhere, your first step is to cast off. It's the only way to get from here to there.

> **Good-Living Principle 71:**
> **WISE UP by moving on.**

Optional Exercises

1. Are you a free spirit able to live and work in the present? Or are you tied to the past and afraid of the future? Respond to these questions in your journal.

2. Do a research paper on one or more techniques to "be here now."

3. Write yourself a letter on how you might overcome some obstacle in your life.

72 Go Within

> The kingdom of God is within you.
> *Luke 17:21*

Seeing, we say, is believing. So, in the West and especially America, if you can't see, feel, taste, smell, or touch something, it probably doesn't exist. Strangely, the United States has a very high rate of people who believe in God.

But this reading isn't about the existence of God. Rather, it's about the importance of the inner life. By that, we don't mean thinking and certainly not worrying. Rather, that inner temple of silence where you can become calm despite outward concerns.

No matter how bad a storm over the ocean may be, if you go deep enough, you'll find still water. The same is true of us. No matter how turbulent our outer situation, somewhere within we will find calm.

This fact has led humankind to devise an array of spiritual "diving" techniques appealing to different types of people. Prayers or passages of Scripture—the 23rd Psalm or the Buddhist Refuge Prayer comes to mind—can bring people to tranquility. Some individuals seek out Nature. Even sports and other vigorous physical activity can help.

Saints, they say, are always in that place, despite how engaged in this world they may seem. "Outwardly active, inwardly quiet" is how the Javanese proverb puts it.

Given accelerating change, the 21st Century will provide plenty of turbulence. People who live well will be those who can refresh themselves by finding their inner refuge.

> **Good-Living Principle 72:**
> **WISE UP by regularly going within.**

Optional Exercises

1. Do you have some favorite techniques for "entering your inner temple"? Describe them in your journal.

2. Discuss with a classmate or friend what causes you to lose your cool.

3. Try a new quieting exercise for a week; then write about the results.

73 Curb Your Desires

> Decrease your wants; fulfill your needs.
> *Mohandas K. Gandhi*

Desire is natural, but unlimited desire is unhealthy. We go to McDonald's and supersize the French fries and the drink. Today, there are more shopping malls in the United States than high schools. We have multiple cars, closets full of clothes, and girl or boy friends galore. Things that used to be luxuries have become necessities. We believe more is better. We cling to our desires as though they were our best friends.

The market and media don't help. They continuously urge us to increase our consumption. Credit cards are issued even when not requested or when someone has not managed his or her debt responsibly. Not surprisingly, credit-card indebtedness now rivals the national debt. The average American is armed with plastic and can be presumed dangerous, to him- or herself.

By contrast, happiness comes from living within our means. If we don't learn to curb our desires, we end up pursuing unobtainable goals. The result is obvious: perennial dissatisfaction. On the other hand, by dealing with this obsession effectively, we will be able to balance our material and spiritual lives.

Limiting our desires does not mean turning our backs on worldly things. Instead it means pursuing our desires in moderation while feeling no inclination to hoard or attach more meaning to possessions or physical comforts than they can bear. Containing our wants will lead to contentment. And contentment is another word for happiness.

> **Good-Living Principle 73:**
> **WISE UP by limiting your desires.**

Optional Exercises

1. Are you suffering from consumerism? Outline the details in your journal.

2. If yes, list areas where you are going beyond sensible limits.

3. Identify and discuss in your journal three ways you might simplify your life.

74 Learn a Trade

> Give me a fish and I'll eat for a day; teach me to fish and I'll eat for a lifetime.
>
> *Chinese saying*

This tip is self-explanatory. Still, many of us don't make the effort when young to learn a trade or develop the skills to help us earn a living. We may have ideas of what kind of work we'd like to do. But ideas are not enough. Plans for getting a good job or starting a successful business are valuable only when acted upon, and it's hard to act effectively without the needed knowledge and training.

Having the skill set to take charge of our financial destiny without relying on outside factors such as a stable and growing job market will be vital as the new century unfolds. Becoming an effective entrepreneur may well be the main factor in achieving personal success and happiness in tomorrow's uncertain world. Especially in materially less developed countries, the capacity to create and exploit opportunities will be essential for surviving and thriving, not to mention building up the countries themselves.

How sad if we can't provide for our family, educate our kids, help the poor, and, not least, earn enough to care for our own financial needs! So start early to learn how to make a decent living. You'll be glad later on.

> **Good-Living Principle 74:**
> **WISE UP by learning to be**
> **financially sustainable.**

Optional Exercises

1. What skills do you have to help you make a decent living? Now, identify additional skills that may benefit you.

2. Write a paper on the effect of your financial affairs on other areas of your life.

3. Interview the most financially successful person you know. Write up what you learn.

Be Honest

There are white lies and black ones. There is white magic and black magic. But magic, white or black, is still magic. And lies, regardless of the intention, are still lies.

Mark Twain put it best. Liars, he said, need good memories. Once you get started in a lie, you need to make sure you keep your "facts" straight and tell everyone the same story.

A good liar, in short, has to be perfect—a tall order for most of us.

Once, when one of us was a teenager, he attended a school where he was younger than his classmates. At that time in New York State, the legal drinking age was 18. Because of the sophistication gained from the older boys, he was able to pass for 18 and drink beer with his friends. One day at his parents' country club, he volunteered to be hypnotized by an entertainer and, without wanting to, told his true age (15). The bartenders were watching. Thus ended our young man's underage drinking career at that club.

Getting caught in this lie was embarrassing. Besides the bartenders, he had also told a few young ladies he was 18. Thus he learned a lesson he never forgot.

The point is clear. To live well in this or any century, honesty is the best policy.

> **Good-Living Principle 75:**
> **WISE UP by being honest.**

Optional Exercises

1. Have you ever been caught in a lie? Journal about what you learned from the experience.

2. Is it ever justifiable to tell a lie? Discuss this question in class or with a friend.

3. Is telling only part of the truth the same as lying? Write an essay pro or con.

Be Loyal

76

> If disloyalty is shameful even in dogs, how can it be right in human beings?
>
> *Jalaluddin Rumi, Turkish Sufi poet, 1207-1273*

The dictionary describes loyalty as faithfulness to a government, friend, or oath. In short, keeping one's word. The English *loyal* is related to the French *loi*, or "law." There's a sense of obligation, especially in an oath, to do what you've promised.

Disloyalty can be dangerous. We all know of cases where officials have been dismissed from office or even killed as traitors for having been disloyal to their leader. Dictators are fanatical in their need for loyalty. Hitler and Stalin are merely among more recent examples of this syndrome.

Of course, it makes sense to be loyal to those persons who have been loyal to us—our parents, for example. They have gone through the trouble of bringing us into the world; feeding, clothing, and sheltering us; passing along their values and beliefs; and often sacrificing their own pleasure to give us a superior education, travel, or other opportunities for personal growth.

Loyalty to country, or patriotism, is universal. "Sweet and fitting it is to die for one's country," the Roman poet Horace wrote 2,000 years ago. Two millennia later, many Americans echo this sentiment with "Right or wrong, my country!" But if your highest loyalty is to truth or justice, sometimes lesser loyalties must give way—a choice requiring certainty, courage, and sometimes one's life.

> **Good-Living Principle 76:**
> **WISE UP by being appropriately loyal.**

Optional Exercises

1. How loyal are you to your friends and family? Journal on this topic.

2. Is loyalty sometimes a vice? Discuss this question with a friend or classmate.

3. If you were ordered to kill for your country, would you? Why? Why not?

Take Responsibility

77

> The price of greatness is responsibility.
> *Sir Winston Churchill, 1874-1965*

Small children when they break something will say "My hand did it." They know they are in for a scolding. At the very least, their parents will be sad—especially if the object had sentimental or financial value.

Being answerable for our actions is a sign of maturity. The Latin saying puts it bluntly: We are the authors of our own disasters.

Of course, we are sometimes only the co-authors. Many actions have multiple causes. In others, luck may play a role.

We may be sitting in our car at a stoplight when the car behind us fails to slow down and rear-ends us. Maybe the driver was distracted. Maybe he or she was driving under the influence of alcohol. Maybe the person in question was a new driver who hit the brakes too late.

It's inappropriate to take responsibility for a mistake that was beyond our control. We are sometimes the victim of someone else's action, period.

There are mistakes of omission as well as commission. In many U.S. states, drivers who fail to stop and render assistance at the site of an accident have committed a misdemeanor. Bottom line: As mature people, we must be prepared to answer for both what we do and what we fail to do. The world and our conscience demand no less.

> **Good-Living Principle 77:**
> **WISE UP by taking responsibility for your actions.**

Optional Exercises

1. How objective are you in taking responsibility for your actions or inactions? Write on this topic in your journal.

2. Discuss with a friend an instance in which a country wrongly refused responsibility for something.

3. Write an official and suggest how s/he might claim a misdeed and move on.

78 Do Good

> Do all the good
> you can, / By all
> the means you
> can, / In all the
> ways you can, /
> In all the places
> you can, / At all
> the times you
> can, / To all the
> people you can,
> / As long as ever
> you can.
>
> *John Wesley, Founder
> of Methodism,
> 1703-1791*

Doing good has gotten a bad reputation in the West. Expressions like *do-gooder* or *goody-goody* are terms of scorn. We are suspicious of the motives of someone who insists on doing one good deed after another. There must be something negative behind all this conspicuous benevolence.

"The person who is always nice is not always nice," say the Poles. Beware the face that smiles too much!

How sad! Yet we live in a world where you can't be too careful. The person knocking at your door might be a confidence man, rapist, or worse.

The earlier tradition is nicer. It urges us to do all the good we can on the logical assumption that if more of us would do good, the world would become a better place for everyone. The Prophet Muhammad's cousin and son-in-law, Ali (c. 600-661 C.E.), said, "To make one good action succeed another is the perfection of good-ness." Eleven hundred years later, a Mennonite Christian proverb advises, "Do good and leave behind you a monument of virtue the storms of time can never destroy."

While it is sensible to be careful, it is wise to follow this advice.

Good-Living Principle 78: WISE UP by doing good.

Optional Exercises

1. Journal about someone who purported to do good but was actually intent on doing evil.

2. Write an essay about a genuinely good human being you know.

3. The Boy Scout Oath requires doing a good deed every day. Do you? Should you?

79 Laugh

> Laughter is the sun that drives winter from the human face.
>
> *Victor Hugo*

And, we might add, the human heart. Abraham Lincoln once said, "With the fearful strain that is on me night and day, if I did not laugh I should die."

A German proverb similarly states, "When we are born, the people around us laugh while we cry. We should so live that when we die, we can laugh while the people around us cry."

Laughter ventilates our heart and soul. Without laughter, daily existence would be too heavy. As the Existentialist philosophers of the 20th Century liked to point out, we have all been found guilty and are under a death sentence. Life itself is terminal.

Laughter makes the burden of that knowledge bearable and keeps us in the game of daily living. It breaks through the cloud cover of depression like the sun and turns the gray skies blue. It keeps the devil and all his helpers at bay. In fact, it drives them and the bad thoughts they plant in us away. For if there is one thing the diabolical forces can't stand, it's a human being who likes to laugh.

The Javanese of Indonesia say that people who laugh frequently won't get cancer. Whether or not this is true is less important than the principle involved. As a recent American proverb puts it, "The person who laughs, lasts."

> **Good-Living Principle 79:**
> **WISE UP by remembering to laugh.**

Optional Exercises

1. Are you a good laugher, or do you tend to take everything seriously? Analyze your R (risibility) Factor in your journal.

2. Observe the best laugher you know. Then, try to emulate his/her approach to life.

3. Spend five minutes each morning for a week visualizing yourself laughing.

80 Dance

> Dancing is the loftiest, the most moving, the most beautiful of the arts, because it is no mere translation or abstraction from life; it is life itself.
> *Havelock Ellis, 1859-1939*

Life, the Hindus say, is a cosmic dance. Vishnu, divinity as Preserver, is often depicted as a dancer. So is Shiva, god as Destroyer.

Contemporary physics sees life as a dance too—a random movement of energy. It's hard to imagine that everything we see, hear, feel, taste, or smell is really invisible motion. Our desk is merely the momentary creation of a bunch of electricity interacting with itself—energy dancing so fast it seems solid, like the realities of the Holodeck in *Star Trek*. Turn the computer off, and everything disappears.

As Prospero says in Shakespeare's *Tempest*, "Our revels now are ended. These our actors, / As I foretold you, were all spirits, and / Are melted into air, into thin air…. / We are such stuff / As dreams are made on, and our little life / Is rounded with a sleep."

But if that is so, we too must dance.
As Alexis Zorba teaches his young boss
in Kazantzakis's novel, dancing is our
traditional medicine against insanity.
Every indigenous people dances. Dancing
gets us out of our heads and into our
bodies. Like dervishes, we must whirl
our way through life to the music of the
spheres. Only death stands still.

> **Good-Living Principle 80:**
> **WISE UP by dancing frequently.**

Optional Exercises

1. Do you like to dance? Reflect on
   and write an essay about your
   relationship to dancing.

2. Take a course on movement or
   dance and journal on the experience.

3. See *Zorba the Greek* or *Black
   Orpheus*; then write about the role
   of dancing in the movie you saw.

Conclusion—
Farewell to our readers

Even in Mecca people make money.
WEST AFRICAN SAYING

Dear Youth,

Here is our final advice for leading the good life: Work for balance.

Extremes are easy. Getting the right balance is hard but necessary.

Take the demands of the material versus the spiritual life. Some cultures have decided that you can do only one or the other well. If you want to make it in this world, focus there. If you want to be truly spiritual, live apart.

In the 21st Century we'll need to learn to live successfully in the material world without neglecting our spirituality and to be spiritual without becoming ineffective in everyday life.

Striving for balance in other areas is also important. For instance, how to attend to our families and friends without neglecting our work; how to include good food, enough sleep, exercise, and leisure in long days at work; how to integrate our male and female sides; even, how to weigh the claims of all people as people against the need for rewarding individual excellence.

We must also balance preparation with spontaneity and the growing glut of information with the need to find meaning.

We do not live by head alone but have bodies, feelings, and souls. All these instruments require care. If any is

deprived at the expense of the others, our *yin* and *yang*—those complementary opposites of Chinese philosophy—get out of synch, and the good life remains beyond our reach.

Best wishes as you take your place in the world. By applying the principles in this book, you should be able to live a truly good life: One that fulfills your dreams while enriching those around you, including Mother Earth.

Aloha,

Reynold Feldman and M. Jan Rumi

Acknowledgments

When eating a fruit, think of the person
who planted the tree.
Vietnamese Saying

Much of the wisdom in this book, to the extent that you
have found some, comes from somewhere else. Just like
the Vietnamese proverb quoted above. We as authors
resemble servers in a restaurant. We didn't cook the food
and certainly didn't grow it. We simply brought it from
the kitchen to your table. Let's hope you found it tasty,
nourishing, and hot. At the very least, it should have been
what you ordered.

So, to begin with, we thank our parents for bearing us
and bearing with us, for educating and having faith in
us. We thank our siblings for allowing us to be ourselves,
even when that meant being different from them. We
thank our teachers, both formal and informal, for helping
us become more of the persons we were meant to be. We
thank our colleagues and associates for making do with
less of us than in the past because we were "busy with the
book." Mostly, though, we thank our spouses and children, who undoubtedly bore the brunt of our authorship
in more ways than one.

As for the book itself, we need to acknowledge our graph-
ic-design consultant, Ms. Giselle Palacios DelMundo, now
of New York City, for her innovative design work and
for patiently and quickly dealing with our latest changes—even though the prior set was supposed to have been
the last. In this regard, thanks go as well to Ms. Christine

Feldman for suggesting some of the key design elements before we had the good fortune of finding Giselle.

We'd also like to acknowledge Mr. Welmon "Rusty" Walker, Jr., publisher and consultant to publishers, for keeping us focused on marketing this book. Writing, for Rusty, is only half the job, or less. Getting it into the hands of enthusiastic readers is where most independent publishers fail—something Rusty was dedicated to prevent in our case. Let's hope he was successful. In this context, thanks to Ms. Palacios DelMundo once again and Mr. Walker for helping us put together a creditable and (we hope) effective website—www.WisingUp.com.

Thanks to the young people at the Second International Varindra T. Vittachi Conference in Crestone, Colorado, as well as those at the World Congress of Youth, Morocco, for reviewing a pre-publication edition of *WisingUp* and, in many cases, providing us with feedback and statements of endorsement. The same is true for a number of adult youth workers and teachers. Above all, we are extremely grateful to Wally Amos, entrepreneur, writer, philanthropist, and renowned cookie-maker, who stole time from a very busy schedule to provide a thoughtful Foreword.

As we look to international distribution of this book, we would like to thank the following persons for their assistance and encouragement: Mr. Philip Wang, chair of Commercial Press Ltd., Taiwan, and Ms. Megan Yu, deputy editor-in-chief; Ms. Ihsan Messaoudi of the Moroccan Youth Forum; Mr. Driss Guerraoui, advisor to the Prime Minister of Morocco; Drs. Richard and Eriko Hogeboom of Honolulu and Nara, Japan; Ms. Mary Matayoshi, executive director of the Volunteer

Resource Center of Hawaii; Mr. Sharif and Mrs. Isniastuti Horthy of the Guerrand-Hermès Foundation for Peace, Lewes, England; Dr. Werner Greis, president of UnitedGames International of Graz, Austria; Mr. Ziga Vavpotic, director of the Slovenian Youth Association, Ljubljana, Slovenia; and Mr. David and Mrs. Rosie Woollcombe, president and executive director, respectively, of Peace Child International, Buntingford, England.

Not least, we want to thank you, our readers, for taking the time to see if we had anything valuable to offer. Let's hope we did and do. When you have a moment, drop us a line at info@WisingUp.com and help us wise up as we contemplate our next collaborative writing project.

Finally, each of us in his own way and tradition would like to thank Almighty God, without whom (we believe) there would have been no world, no authors, no readers, and no book.

WisingUp Book Order Form

By Reynold Feldman & and M. Jan Rumi
Foreword By Wally Amos
ISBN 1-932590-02-1, 5 x 8" 192 Pages
Wisdom Foundation Publishing
P.O. Box 61599, Honolulu, HI 96839-1599 USA
Order@WisingUp.com

Shipping by US Mail is FREE. Complete this order form and send it with your check or signed charge card information to Wisdom Foundation Publishing.

Please send me _____ WisingUp books at **$15.00** each. I understand that shipping and handling is FREE for 1 to 4 books send to the same address. The total price for this order is $_____

Print Your Name_____

Address_____

City _____State ____Zip____

Country _____E-mail _____
Visa ___MasterCard ___

Number _____
Expiration Date on card _____

_____
Signature of card holder